BEACHCOMBING AND CAMPING

ALONG THE NORTHWEST COAST

The Cover Picture: Dale Brien Webber, a son of the authors, posed for this photograph on Dec. 2, 1972, near Bandon, Oregon. *See*: pp. 72-73.

The Endsheet Picture: Looking north from the head at Port Orford, Oregon. Cape Blanco on horizon.

BEACHCOMBING
and CAMPING
along the NORTHWEST COAST

BERT & MARGIE WEBBER

YE GALLEON PRESS
Fairfield, Washington
1978

✳   ✳   ✳   ✳

Ye Galleon Press
Fairfield, Washington
99012

Library of Congress Cataloging in Publication data:

Webber, Bert
  Beachcombing and camping along the Northwest coast.

  Bibliography: p.
  Includes index.
    1. Beachcombing—Northwest. Pacific. 2. Camping—
Northwest. Pacific.
I. Webber, Margie, joint author. II. Title.
G532.5.N95W43   917.95'044   78-4639

ISBN O-87770-192-x
ISBN O-87770-162-8 pbk.

iv

TABLE OF CONTENTS

Continued on next page —

Bert and Margie Webber on Siletz (Salishan) Spit.

INTRODUCTION

The authors engage in numerous hobbies and have always been enthusiastic readers. If we had to choose which activity we like the best, we would pick beachcombing and the travel associated with it.

Beachcombing can be done in any kind of weather. "The tide [and wind] hindereth no man," wrote John Heywood (1497-1580), but we are not out to trudge through the worst storms just to say we did it. We enjoy the creature-comforts and often plan our trips with them in mind.

Day-campers miss a lot by not hanging around for nightfall for at night concerts of sounds issue from the sea. Waves crash with sforzando impact upon the shore. The metallic blast of fog horns can be likened to trombones while the counterpoint of clanking bell buoys gives way to the WWOOOOOaaaaaaaph of

the mournful deepthroated whistling buoy. As has been written, to be inside a tin-top camper on a stormy night is like being inside a snare drum during a Sousa March. We enjoy reading about the shores along the North Pacific Rim then when practical, visit as many of them as we can. We remember our excursions with pictures, notes and trophies. (From these we sometimes develop books.)

How fortunate for us that we have been able to beachcomb the Northwest Coast, California, parts of Alaska, the major Micronesian Islands, Okinawa and the Ichinomiya Prefecture shore of Japan. Hopefully we will complete the North Pacific Rim with beach explorations of the Aleutians, Kamchatka and Baja.

In the present volume we offer our experiences to "master" beachcombers, as well as to newcomers, to the restfully-exciting activity of beachcombing and camping along the Northwest Coast.

Bert and Margie Webber
Central Point, Oregon
March 1978

CHAPTER 1

WHY BEACHCOMB ?

People talk so much about beachcombing for driftwood, fishing floats, foreign bottles, and for the remains of broken ships, that sometimes we become enmeshed in these extrinsics and miss something else: a serenity that some capture just walking on the beach.

There is something to be gained after a walk on the beach whether one comes home with a shining glass fishing float, or comes away having found peace within himself and ready for a fresh look at the responsibilities of everyday life.

Recently a person lost employment after working for a firm for many years. What to do? He went to the beach and soaked up some sun while he sorted out his priorities. "Men are polished...as pebbles are smoothed on the rolling beach," wrote John Townsend Trowbridge (1827-1916).

A couple may find togetherness while beachcombing. They might walk hundreds of yards without saying a word and might not even be walking close together. Their thoughts are their own. The continuous pounding of the breakers deadens all other sounds along the beach. The awesome sea — the immeasureable power of the sea. Philosophers, engineers, scientists, fishermen — in fact men of all disciplines have studied the sea for centuries just trying to discover its secrets. Whatever its secrets, the sounds and sights of the sea often mellow men to better understanding.

Probably the majority of those who walk on the beach pick up something to take home with them. For many years there have been those who search for salvageable material that they can sell. Of more recent years are those who are looking for collectables with which to decorate their homes or to make things with.

Those who really know the beaches of the rugged Northwest Coast claim the best hunting is during the winter months. It is really an experience to trudge over the sand, rocks, and driftwood with a swift offshore wind blowing sand that strikes unprotected parts of the body like millions of tiny darts. Hiking into the wind on

the way *out* from the camp site makes for an easy return when the blasting is then at one's heels. (If you are carrying a load of "trophies" from the beach, the tail-wind seems helpful!)

Back at camp, after a bowl of steaming chili or soup, it is an experience to huddle inside a sleeping bag and drift off to sleep while the rain pounds on a tin-roofed trailer. It has been said that the rain's tattoo during a Northwest Coast winter storm is like being inside a snare drum during a Sousa march! Some beachside motel operators advertise that one can not truly appreciate the Northwest Coast until one experiences a night during a winter storm.

The highest tides of the year smack the land during the winter months. When the wind is right, thunderous, pounding breakers crash against seawalls and sometimes drive huge logs through the windows of beach homes and motels built too close to the water. In December 1967, what was called by the press "the most damaging storm of the decade," driven by 100-mile-per-hour gusts, hurled logs and other debris across Highway 101 in several locations. And there are more recent examples of a winter storm's fury when in 1973 a house, being constructed on Siletz (Salishan) Spit, crumbled to the beach below when breakers collapsed a sand dune upon which the house was perched.

In February 1976 again King Neptune roared in with knockout blows at anything in his way—sent people to the hospital who had been cut by flying glass when waves caved in a window at a beachside restaurant.

But along with the fury of the storm come delicate, foreign-made glass fish

(Top) February sunset at Cannon Beach, Oregon. (bottom) Discarded spark plug with crust of hardened sand and small rocks. Beachcombed at Newport, Oregon.

Refreshment on a hot summer day on the south Oregon coast.

net floats and light bulbs, as well as bottles, agates, sand dollars, driftwood and whatall, and a sign of the age—a litter of plastic!

Once the winds die and the walking becomes safe, beachcombers head for tide lines with pack sack over shoulder. It is at this point where one must make a decision. What are you looking for? Are you a specialist in your beachcombing? Do you want glass floats only? Agates? Are you after driftwood for your home's fireplace—better get a beach driving permit and bring your fourwheel drive truck—or small intricate pieces for making into driftwood sculpture? Although there is some specialization by curio shop operators seeking glass floats, a true beachcomber, the local people claim, picks up anything that seems interesting when they come upon it. (They'll decide what to do with it later.)

Beachcombing along the Northwest Coast can be rewarding in different ways for different people. And one does not have to beachcomb in the middle of a winter tempest. Whatever time of year one chooses for beachcombing, the Northwest Coast is an exciting arena for the experience. □

Cape Lookout State Park

CHAPTER 2

WHAT IS CAMPING ALL ABOUT ?

It was not so many years back when to be called a "camper" could mean one who existed only on the barest essentials and moved from place to place on foot. A camper was often looked on as an "eccentric" or "nature lover."

Camping has long been associated with the military. To camp, applying a military term of the sixteenth century, meant a place where troops were lodged in tents. But one could apply the term "camping" to the nomadic tribes of the Old Testament who lived in tents also.

Probably the earliest and most extensive camping trip in the history of the United States (and at government expense), was the Lewis and Clark Expedition from the Mississippi River to the Oregon Coast and back (1804-1806).

During the American Civil War, Walter Kittredge, a man who failed to pass the physical examination for the Union Army so had to stay at home, wrote a song about camping, "Tenting Tonight On The Old Camp Ground." In his song, Kittredge envisioned soldiers in bivouac thinking of home and, "wishing for the war to cease...."

It was at this time that the first organized boys groups went camping. They stayed out overnight and they cooked their food over open fires with supervision. During nightly "campfires," they told stories and sang songs. Not long afterward, someone decided that camping would be a good sport for girls too. Now, organized

Four-wheeled semi-selfcontained family camper of
late 18th century.

camping groups such as the Boy and Girl Scouts, Camp Fire Girls, and numerous others, offer outdoor, overnight programs teaching useful skills and coaching self-assurance and responsibility.

There were periods in American history when vagabonds, nearly always men, lived in the "jungles" — camped — near railroad tracks. Later, persons of both sexes called "hippies" camped here and there in protest against "the establishment" — opting out from the ways of life of their parents. In the 1970's the hobos are mostly gone. In place of jungles, to a degree, are the communes (camps ?) of the hippies.

Tens of thousands of infantrymen of the world wars swore on their being discharged, that they would never again sleep on the ground. And many never did. But by the mid-1950's, strides were being made in interstate highway construction and better designs for trailers and campers. Discharged soldiers, and of course many others, watching the great expansion of parks for weekend camping declared, "This is for me!" — thus the era of "tin-can-on-wheels" camping began.

To go camping was once throught to be strictly for men and boys. Dad and his sons would plan for days, then when the weekend rolled around they rolled with it to a fishing hole. Mom became housebound. She rebelled at being left behind so it was not long before women were seen wheeling heavily loaded station wagons pulling trailers into camping areas also. But too often once the outfit was parked, off went the fellows with their fishing rods as before. Mom was left behind with the chores. Some complained, "If I have to cook, wash dishes, clean the camp and fight bugs — then start all over again to get the next meal — I might as well stay at home and be comfortable."

Camper manufacturers must have had some inkling into these situations for

their designers were looking at the history of family travel. They were searching for ways to modernize and market a product that would become a moneymaker for them.

Four-wheel family units, pretty well self-contained, had written a part of American history. Although never noted for speed, those ponderous prairie schooners covered the distance.

Imagine the facial expression of the Chairman of the Board at "Modern Tin-Can Camper Mfg. Co. (Inc.)," when a bright young, think-tank graduate beams, *Modernize the covered wagon!*

A dead silence floats over the room but only for a minute. Here was the genesis of an idea! Motorized units had been built before but they were specialized. These would be mass-produced thus bringing the price down. The old

covered wagon did not have a hot shower, propane stove, electric refrigerator and television, but the new "recreational vehicle" would have!

Madison Avenue's advertising kings could not bear up under such a long handle as REC-REE-AA-SHUN-VEE-ICK-UL. Somebody must have commanded: "Shorten it!" In no time at all just plain R-VEE has become a household word.

Camping in the 1970's can generally be defined as the act of living away from home and spending nights in the open *for fun*. Millions are doing it and some travel great distances to do so.

Oregon was the first state to provide highway "Safety Rest Areas" where motorists can rest for as many as eighteen hours in any twenty-four hour period. Come dusk, drivers, particularly in the summer months, sometimes have trouble finding a place to park in some of these freeway sidings which may be already filled with overnight "resters." It is unlawful to pitch a tent in a Safety Rest Area in Oregon, or to create unnecessary noise, or to let pets run loose. Since the state created these

(Pg. 14) Some contemporary campers are built on truck chassis. Weight and design (airflow) are factors for determining ride comfort and operation costs. (Pg. 15 top) Light weight fiberglass camper, small and efficient, has little effect on gasoline mileage, sleeps four. Unit shown had just arrived at Pelican Beach, California, from Canada via Washington and Oregon Coast Highway. (Bottom) Heavily constructed travel trailers of 1950's are often used by hunters and fishermen as on-site "headquarters." Trailer shown is at public campsite at Port of Brookings, Harbor, Oregon.

15

One of the beaches along the Olympic National Park beach strip.

The Washington Coast facing the Pacific Ocean, is approximately two hundred miles long. Of this, about half is sand beach suitable for beachcombing. In Oregon, the coast line is nearly four hundred miles in length with all but one short section, and some isolated points totaling about ten per cent, sandy beach. The area in California is just under eighty miles extending from the Oregon border. Of this, nearly eighty per cent is walkable beach.

The northern half of coastal Washington is of rocky cliffs and short beaches. A forty-five mile section of this area is under the jurisdiction of the Olympic National Park. Camping regulations and maps are included in an information packet available from park headquarters, Port Angeles, Washington 98362. Few roads enter the area and no motor vehicles are permitted on the trails or beaches within the National Park.

There is excellent beachcombing along the National Park strip. At Lake Ozette, the six miles round trip hike can consume the better part of a day.

During World War II the Coast Guard operated a large number of Beach Patrol stations along the west coast of the United States. The patrolmen were on the alert for possible enemy landings. To be stationed at Lake Ozette, La Push, or other spots along this part of the coast was cause for much grousing. In the fall of 1942, a husky Guardsman shouldered a one hundred pound iron cookstove and packed it non-stop to the beach. This was before the trail was improved.

Campers and beachcombers desiring to visit the northwest Washington coast are reminded that the Makah, Ozette and Quinault Indians prohibit non-Indians from trespassing on Reservation beaches. (See APPENDIX for regulations.)

The Makah Reservation includes Cape Flattery. A public trail is maintained to the end of the cape where there is an historical marker. The Ozette Reservation

NO BEACHCOMBING HERE!
According to the Indians, non-Indians have damaged Reservation beaches to point where non-Indians are presently excluded from Tribal Beaches.
Violators may be forceably ejected and may be brought before Tribal Council.
(*See*: Notes, Chapter 3.)

is near Cape Alava. Cape Alava is the westernmost *point* of the forty-eight contiguous states and is about thirteen miles south of Cape Flattery. The Quinault Reservation is the largest of the three and extends from north of Queets to south of Point Grenville near the town of Moclips.

La Push, at the mouth of the Quillayute (*QUILL-ee-yoot*) River, is the westernmost *town* in the forty-eight contiguous states. Just south of La Push is Quillayute Needle, a nearly vertical rock about thirty-five feet wide and eighty-one feet high.

In this most northwesterly region the annual rainfall is extreme with over 140 inches in a year spread over about 210 days. Even in July there are a relatively small total number of hours of sunshine. The winds are westerly and northwesterly in summer, and when it is not raining, intense fog may persist for days—especially between July and September—the usual vacation and camping months.

South of Taholah, the beaches widen and there are fewer rocky promontories than are found to the north. State Highway 109, from the south, terminates at Taholah (where there is an Indian village), but parallels the beach to Ocean City. In this mid-section of the Washington Coast, referred to as "Olympic Beaches," there are numerous small towns, camp grounds and resorts and lots of sandy beaches to explore. The beach continues south along a spit ending at Point Brown

Mouth
Kalaloch River

beyond the community of Ocean Shores. The spit is wide, flat, and yields excellent beachcombing trophies.

Across the entrance of Grays Harbor from Point Brown is Point Chehalis near the town of Westport. The twelve mile coastal strip south to Cape Shoalwater is called "Twin Harbor Beaches" and is along a fine sandy ocean frontage. Although the weather picture improves as one moves south, this area, particularly close to North Cove is subject to severe weather and is erosion-prone during winter storms.

Willapa Bay separates Cape Shoalwater from Leadbetter Point. From the point, a broad, almost flat beach about twenty-eight miles long called "Long Beach Peninsula," extends to near the city of Ilwaco. This beach is probably the world's longest continuous stretch of sand beach. The peninsula is accessible by motor vehicles only from the south. This beach, and many others along the Northwest Coast, may be driven on by automobiles and light campers within certain regulations. Rules for beach driving are posted a each access road.

To the southwest of the peninsula is Cape Disappointment. The cape is composed of a group of rounding hills, about two-and-one-half miles long and one mile wide, divided by a narrow valley extending to the northwest. The ocean side of the camp is precipitous cliffs with jagged, rocky points and small strips of sand

Low tide at Moclips.

Low tide at Cape Disappointment.

beach. Although the area has three distinct "heads," McKenzie Head, North Head, and Cape Disappointment, all three are generally included within the name, "Cape Disappointment" when used for non-navigational purposes. North Head is the highest of the three (270 feet), and it is at the extreme western end. The Coast Guard maintains light houses on both North Head and on Cape Disappointment. (Appendix F)

McKenzie Head, in the middle, was used by the 249th Coast Artillery (Oregon National Guard) during World War II as a searchlight position. On the night of June 21, 1942, the men on duty on McKenzie Head and Cape Disappointment had what might be called, "high-angle ring side seats" from which to watch the Japanese submarine *I-25* shoot its deck gun in the direction of Fort Stevens to the south.

On a clear day, one standing on North Head can see the entire length of Long Beach Peninsula.

As will be noted on a map, a substantial part of the Washington Coast has no access for motor vehicles because of lack of roads and Indian and National Park

Looking north from Astoria—Megler Bridge near mouth of Columbia River in January. Expect heavier traffic in summer.

"Squirrelling" on beach may leave interesting patterns in the sand, but beaches are patrolled and such driving techniques can bring citations

restrictions. By way of contrast, the Oregon Coast has much beach access to the public because Highway 101 (Oregon Coast Highway) parallels the coast almost the entire length of the state. When this main route turns inland, local roads are available. The northerly eighty per cent of the Oregon coast is sandy beach except for a few promontories. The Siuslaw (sseye-YOO-slaw) National Forest, offering dozens of camp sites, borders the ocean for many miles. Oregon has no National Park along the coast.

On entering Oregon at the Astoria Bridge, newcombers might want to stop and look over the array of travel folders and maps in the Visitor's Information Office at the end of the bridge ramp. (At this writing, the state operates this office only during summer months.) The Official Oregon highway map includes a color code along the left margin (the ocean frontage) denoting the status of beaches for use by motor vehicles. In short, some beaches have a total restriction against motor vehicles while other are open on a seasonal basis. Some are open all year. Oregon beaches are part of the Oregon State Highway System and are regularly patrolled.

For those entering Oregon from the south, there is a Visitor's Information Office at the Safety Rest Area just north of Brookings, on the east side of the highway. (At this writing, the State operates this office only during summer.)

See: Chapter 4.
"A Close Look at the
Oregon Coast."

The weather for the Oregon Coast varies considerably. There is more rain near the Columbia River than at mid-coast, and still less at the southern extreme. Whereby the northwest corner of Washington is noted for rain forests and Mount Olympus (7,965 feet elevation), the highest rain-beckoning peaks in Northwest

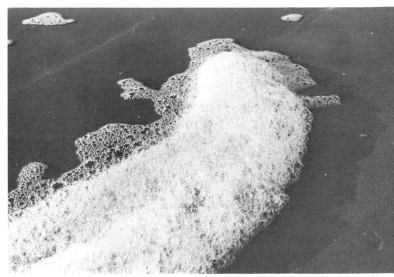

Foam from a crashing breaker.

Oregon are considerably less than half this height.

The Oregon Dunes Recreation Area was recently created by the Federal Government. The famous dunes extend from near Florence, at the mouth of the Siuslaw River, to Coos Bay, a distance of about fifty miles. The beachcombing is good. There are "for hire" dune buggy rides—a thrill not to be missed—and privately owned buggies may be driven in selected areas.

From Coos Bay south are many fine beaches but steep rocky cliffs become more frequent. Although the end of Cape Blanco is 225 feet high and drops almost straight down to the sea, the beachcombing possibilities immediately north and south of the cape are excellent.

At Port Orford is Battle Rock Wayside. This is a rest area (no camping), and a stop here to read the data on the historical marker is a good excuse for getting out and stretching. Kids love to climb Battle Rock. Most anyone can do it. There is a trail, but going up and down the face of the rock can be tedious for some. At low tide, beach strollers can walk through the short tunnel in Battle Rock.

South of Port Orford, the Oregon Coast is noted for its fantastic views of rocky cliffs and offshore projections that raise straight out of the sea. Along this section are several beaches although many are relatively short.

At the mouth of the Rogue River is the most westerly *city* in the contiguous United States, Gold Beach. For the beachcombing camper who wants to spend a day in a completely different experience, investigate the jet boat "white water" excursions on the river. The starting points for several firms offering such trips are along the river and there are camp grounds nearby. (Most river tours require advance reservations which can usually be made by telephone.)

Immediately south of Gold Beach the highway climbs Cape Sebastian (715 feet elevation) then just as abruptly descends to Pistol River. While the road is wide and of excellent quality, fog can grip at traffic forcing speeds downward to a snail's pace on both approaches to the summit.

Highway 101 from Pistol River south follows the coastline closely to Brookings, while the old road climbs inland and passes the ghost town of

NO LICENSE REQUIRED

TO ANGLE FOR:

SEA PERCH	TOM COD
SMELT	FLOUNDER
HERRING	CRAB

OTHER BOTTOM FISH

ENJOY YOURSELF

(Pg. 24) Sign on north bank at mouth of Rogue River. (Pg. 25, top) Licenses are not required in Oregon for rock and surf fishing.

Carpenterville. At the summit one can look westward over the lower hills to the ocean, and southeasterly to Mount Shasta, California.

The old road rejoins Highway 101 north of Brookings, then the highway continues into California after crossing the Chetco and Winchuck Rivers. The particular lay of the land, for about fifteen miles from Brookings to a point south of the town of Smith River, California, as well as the influence of the warm (winter) alongshore Davidson Current, causes a weather condition unique when compared with the balance of the Northwest Coast. It is frequent that the warmest winter temperature of all of Oregon will be recorded at Brookings. And in summer, the Brookings area may be shrouded in cool fog (while the people in the valleys east of the Coast Range swelter). It is along this strip that approximately ninety per cent of the Easter Lily bulbs marketed in North America originate.

Let us pause to compare some differences between the borders of Washington and Oregon, and Oregon and California.

The border between Washington and Oregon at the coast is the Columbia River. For decades, the four-mile-wide river mouth was a formidable barrier for landlubbers, for it was not until 1921 that a regular ferry service was started. The boats operated between Megler, on the Washington side, which is about ten miles east of Ilwaco at the base of Long Beach Peninsula, and Astoria, Oregon. Although the service on the river was frequent, schedules were interrupted by weather. If travellers were not acquainted with the situation, long waits were inevitable. For an outing from one state to the other and return the same night, it could mean less beachcombing and lots of "camping" in the car waiting for boat space. (Beachcombers in the 1890's from Portland no less, arrived at Ilwaco by river boat and took a train up the peninsula!)

In the mid-1960's, the Astoria-Megler Bridge was opened allowing crossings by car at any time. Gusts of winds of 150 miles per hour, that occasionally batter the coast, still leave the bridge with a safety factor. In addition, the piers of the

bridge are built to withstand the river flood-speed when gigantic whole trees and logs are carried by the raging water.

Crossing the Oregon - California border is quite different—just a continuous stretch of highway and the usual jurisdictional signs. But then a surprise is in store for those who have never previously entered California on a highway from the north or east.

Beginning about 1930, officers of the California State Department of Agriculture, Bureau of Plant Quarantine Inspection Stations, were placed at stations on all highways entering California. They ordered vehicles to stop. These inspections in recent years, on some roads, are reduced to seasonal operation. Although the "bug inspectors" of the "California Customs," as officials and stations are frequently called, pass cars through quickly, if one's picnic basket or camper icebox contains certain fruits, one has a choice of "instant picnic—eat them here," or surrender that part of the lunch to the official. Oregon and Washington grown fresh cherries are generally forbidden entry into California. Likewise citrus fruits, if not clearly established to have been grown in California may not enter. (There are other critical items too numerous to mention here.) The details of such trip interruptions are often exaggerated on being retold, thus many Northwest travelers fear the California border stations and stay on the Oregon side. (There are no inspections when one leaves

California Dept. of Agriculture Inspection Station near Oregon border on Highway 101.

Trailer camping on Oregon's south coast near Winchuck River. *See* **Appendix B for list of campsites.**

California.) The Smith River Inspection Station is a few hundred yards south of the Winchuck River and operates on a seasonal basis.

There is little difference in the ocean frontage on either side of the Oregon - California border. The beach dwindles however, as one continues in a southerly direction. Along the highway are turnouts for parking, each with beach access. Driftwood! In the vicinity of the mouth of the Smith River the beach widens. Access to the Smith River Spit is by rented boat from the north, or by a road from the south. The spit collects driftwood, but fishing floats are rare.

A long, curved beach fronting Pelican Bay is soon noted. The beach narrows, then terminates at Point St. George northwest of Cresent City. Pelican Beach, west of Fort Dick, is somewhat shallow and the drop-off is steep at water's edge. Often one can sit for hours (April—Sept) watching fishermen working the surf with nets for smelt.

Access to Oregon's Rogue Valley (Medford and Interstate Freeway 5) is by way of highway 199 at a junction with the Coast Highway (101) north of Crescent City. On highway 199, those wishing to camp out may want to investigate facilities at Jedediah Smith Redwoods Park (camping summer only—reservations). Situated in a Redwood grove a few miles northeast of Crescent City, the campsites are cooled by the tall trees even on the warmest day these few miles inland, while the coast is shrouded in fog. Unimaginable weather patterns are common along the coast.

South of Crescent City the ocean often beats against cliffs. It is in this area that one enters Redwood National Park (with headquarters in Crescent City). The highway wanders through dense Redwoods for several miles, at times with glimpses of the broad Pacific Ocean through the trees.

For miles here have been advertising signs for "Trees of Mystery," a Commercial entity (fee), alongside the east shoulder of the highway. Weary beachcombing campers will enjoy a break here. The "new" town of Klamath is nearby. At the

Battery Point Lighthouse, Crescent City, now a public museum, is accessible by foot during low tide.

Klamath River, there are roads on each side of the river leading to the mouth. The beaches at the mouth are privately owned and the right to be on these sands may be subject to payment of fees. (Watch for signs.)

The original town of Klamath was washed away by the December 1964 flood. If one looks closely in the marked area along the south bank of the river west of the present bridge, some traces of the former town are yet visible. There is an historical marker on the remains of the Douglas Memorial bridge that was also lost.

A little south of the Klamath River is a county road. Davidson Road leaves the highway on the west. In places the road is steep and limited to one-way traffic. Seek local information before trying an RV on this road which is the only access through a bluff to Gold Bluff Beach State Park (camping all year). Campsites are provided on the beach. Heavy timbers have been installed behind which tents can be set up out of the wind. The beach being fairly flat and long, it should provide some trophies, but driftwood is scarce. This beach is a great place for kids to dig in the sand. (Barefooters need to be alert for flip-rings from pop and beer cans.)

Del Norte (del-nort) Coast Redwoods Park (camping—summer only), is down a steep entry road off the east side of the Coast Highway. Here again the camp site is protected from clammy coastal coolness.

Prairie Creek Redwoods Park (camping—summer only) is off the west side of the highway about four miles south of the town of Klamath. The remnants of a herd of Roosevelt Elk are pastured here.

At Orick, Highway 101 swings again to the ocean frontage. (The world's tallest tree, a Redwood—367.8 feet—stands southwest of the town. An office of the Redwood National Park at Orick has directions and literature.)

Just west of Orick is Lookout Point, from which beachcombers can survey nearly ten miles of ocean frontage immediately in back of which are three large

Redwood Highway at Freshwater Lagoon. Oregon in background.

lagoons. From the north these are Fresh Water Lagoon, Stone Lagoon and Big Lagoon. Dry Lagoon Beach State Park (picnicking—day use only), between Stone and Big Lagoon, makes an excellent headquarters for a day's parking and beachcombing for driftwood, agates and jade. In early summer blackberries are abundant near the park access road. The beach is steep therefore floats seldom land.

The southern limit for our consideration of *Beachcombing and Camping along the Northwest Coast* is at Patrick's Point State Park (camping — summer only). The park sits atop a two-hundred-foot high bluff which juts into the sea on the south of Patrick's Point, with Abalone Beach below. To the northwest, Rocky Point overlooks the long beach that stretches north to Lookout Point. A trail leads down to the beach where heaps of miniature size driftwood await beachcombers.

In the two states and the part of a third included here, there are over 8,000 campsites and hundreds of miles of beaches to prospect. In addition, there are remains of wrecked ships and several operating light houses to investigate either in person, or in books which will be found in most of the libraries along the coast. (Appendix F)

One day a photographer was closely examining a piece of driftwood when some youngsters came up to see what he was doing. One of them volunteered, "We're on vacation and get to stay here for a whole week. It sure is keen on the beach."

The cameraman looked at them. He nodded agreement and thought to himself, "keen" is an interesting way to describe the Northwest Coast, for the only way to really find out about the coast is to visit it. □

CHAPTER 4

A CLOSE LOOK AT THE OREGON COAST

The Oregon seafront is roughly referred to as the North Coast and the South Coast. The North Coast starts at the mouth of the Columbia River and extends to Coos Bay. The area from Coos Bay to the California border is called the South Coast.

Extensive sandy beaches occur mostly in the north region starting at the Columbia River, but as one progresses southward beaches give way to rocky areas and massive headlands. Beaches vary in length and breadth from several miles long to only a dozen yards or so. There are also many rocky shelves and intertidal pools. Near the southern end of the area is the fifty mile long Oregon Dunes National Recreation Area.

The South Coast is noted for many sandy coves alternating with steep rocky outcroppings and intertidal pools on rocky shelves. Often these beaches are accessible only via unimproved trails. Large beaches are few except for a stretch north of Bandon. Possibly the most spectacular part of all of the Northwest Coast is the thirty-five miles between the Rogue River and the Winchuck River near the California border.

NORTH OREGON COAST

Except for the interruption of the Cape Disappointment jut of land and the mouth of the Columbia River, one could say that the broad sand beach of Washington's Long Beach Peninsula continues into Oregon all the way to Tillamook Head.

The beach in Oregon picks up right at the south jetty of the river and is uninterrupted to the Necanicum River at Seaside. From the south bank of the Necanicum the beach continues until it merges with heavy gravel at the base of Tillamook Head. All of this beach can be searched for glass floats, and it is regularly patrolled on foot and with four wheeled vehicles (where permitted) for them. The chances for a visitor to pick up a freshly landed glass ball are rare unless the visitor is on the beach at tide time—which includes being there during the wee hours of the morning. Beachcombers can set up base camp in Fort Stevens State Park (camping all year—reservations in summer).

This long broad beach was one of the locations which was watched with special care during World War II, as the military minds believed it to be a potential invasion beach. Accordingly, today's beachcomber should be on the lookout for war related objects. The 249th Coast Artillery (Oregon National

The Oregon Coast at a Glance

ESTUARIES
1. Columbia River
2. Nehalem River
3. Tillamook Bay
4. Netarts Bay
5. Nestucca River
6. Salmon River
7. Siletz River
8. Yaquina River
9. Alsea River
10. Siuslaw River
11. Umpqua River
12. Coos Bay
13. Coquille River
14. Rogue River
15. Chetco River

HEADLANDS
16. Tillamook Head
17. Cape Falcon
18. Cape Meares
19. Cape Lookout
20. Cape Kiwanda
21. Cascade Head
22. Cape Foulweather
    (Otter Crest)
23. Yaquina Head
24. Cape Perpetua
25. Heceta Head
26. Cape Arago
27. Cape Blanco
28. Cape Sebastian
29. Cape Ferrelo

BEACHES
30. Clatsop Beach
31. Cannon Beach
32. Beverly Beach
33. Agate Beach
34. Bastendorff Beach

COVES
35. Boiler Bay
36. Whale Cove
37. Depoe Bay
38. Sand Lake
39. Sunset Bay
40. Hunters Cove

**OFFSHORE ROCKS
& REEFS**
41. Haystack Rock
    (Cannon Beach)
42. Haystack Rock
    (Pacific City)
43. Stonewall Bank
44. Heceta Bank
45. Rogue River Reef
46. Orford Reef
47. Mack Arch

OTHER LANDMARKS
48. Sea Lion Caves
49. Sand dune area
50. Neahkahnie Mountain
51. Humbug Mountain

ASTORIA
SEASIDE
TILLAMOOK
PACIFIC CITY
LINCOLN CITY
DEPOE BAY
NEWPORT
WALDPORT
YACHATS
FLORENCE
REEDSPORT
COOS BAY
BANDON
PORT ORFORD
GOLD BEACH
BROOKINGS

Fort Stevens
State Park.

Guard) was stationed at Fort Stevens before and during the war. The Guard often held maneuvers and target practice on the beach and in the grass and shrub covered dunes behind the beach. There was a machine gun nest near the remains of the bark *Peter Iredale*. A 75mm gun position was at the base of the south jetty.

In 1976 a beachcomber picked up a 37mm shell. Another retrieved a cymbal, as used in the drum section of a band, from the grassy area. (The cymbal is cracked and is presumed to have been discarded.) One of the workers at the Fort Stevens Historical Research Center found a brass case from one of the 75mm shells.

At the start of the war the entrance of the Columbia River was mined. Some of the mines have "disappeared," according to official records, and are presumed to have broken loose and washed out to sea. Some did. Mines have washed ashore in this area and one was displayed at the 1973 Seaside Beachcombers Festival.

Although some writers, in their enthusiasm, suggest that parts from Japanese submarines, "remains" of Japanese military men and other "enemy" paraphernalia, have been found on the Northwest Coast beaches, if this is so then these items

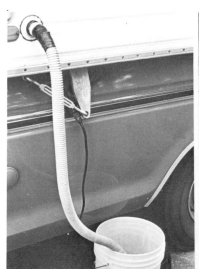

Waste water from *all* RV's must, by law in Oregon, be caught in leak-proof container. (left) Illegal catch bucket. (right) Legal waste water container.

Wartime mine. Note gashes believed caused by passing ship's propeller. (right) 37mm shell. Both beachcombed in 1976 in Oregon near mouth of Columbia River.

would have had to ride in on currents from many miles out — thousands. Documented evidence clearly shows that no Japanese submarines were ever sunk anywhere along the Northwest Coast, and none of their crews were lost overboard here. There were no enemy invasion attempts anywhere along the Northwest Coast although elaborate beach patrols were operated mostly by the Coast Guard. Some of the patrols were mounted — "Join the Coast Guard — Ride a Horse" — and all carried two-way radios.

As has often been pointed out, if one is to find a glass fishing float he must be at the right spot during the right conditions. It can be generally presumed that a visitor to the beach area from Seaside north to the Columbia River, has little chance of picking up a glass ball because of the population density, and the fact that local beachcombers collecting for themselves, or commercially, are on the beach at most every tide.

Nevertheless, during the February 1974 Beachcombers Festival at Seaside, the winds turned, the tide came in, and dozens of persons who had been looking at the festival displays in the Convention Center exited almost on signal and headed for the beach. It was not long before freshly caught floats, new driftwood (and a few objects that did not smell too good), were being hauled into the auditorium by eager, smiling, rainsoaked beach enthusiasts.

Adventurers sometimes hike in areas that are potentially dangerous and this is the situation at the base of Tillamook Head. Although access to Killer Cove can be gained by walking the rocks at low tide from the north, if the tide comes in there is

Oregon beaches are part of State Highway system, and are patrolled regularly. Cannon Beach—Haystack Rock.

The "turnaround," end of Lewis & Clark Trail, Seaside. (top) "Winter" squall strikes about 5 p.m. in August. (bottom) Seaside beach 9 p.m. in summer. Turnaround, left center. Tillamook Head in background.

no escape. The walls of the head are nearly perpendicular and when the tide is high it covers all of the short, narrow beach with up to ten feet of water.

Entry into Ecola State Park (picnicking—trails—day use only), is on a paved road from the north end of the City of Cannon Beach. Ecola State Park is on unstable land and the roads in the area are often closed by land slides. The Indian Beach—Ecola Point areas are exposed to the open sea. Intertidal animals, mainly limited to typical barnacle-mussel beds, star fish and bright green anemone, are found here.

The beach extending south from Elk Creek, in the City of Cannon Beach to the vicinity of Arch Cape is flat and wide. It is a dandy beach for glass float retrieval. Automobiles are permitted to drive on many sections of the beach during certain times of the year and there is good access from a city street in Cannon Beach. At low tide, one can park near Haystack Rock, take position with a camera and shoot professional quality photographs.

Haystack Rock, 235 feet high, is one of the several rock "seastacks" along the Oregon Coast. It is a federal bird refuge so the rock is off limits to climbers. In the

The descriptive plaque nearby tells about the U.S. Naval ship *Shark* which lost this cannon when the ship was wrecked at the mouth of the Columbia River.

early days settlers collected mussels at low tide from Haystack Rock for food when they could not find clams, bear, or elk. (There are two "Haystack Rocks" in this area. Another is off Cape Kiwanda, to the south, which will be mentioned shortly.)

Probably one of the more interesting objects beachcombed along the Northwest Coast came from just south of Tillamook Head. On September 10, 1846, the U.S. Naval ship *Shark* was lost while outcrossing the Columbia River bar. A few weeks later a portion of the ship's deck, to which was attacked a cannon and a capstan, washed ashore about five miles south of Ecola Point. In 1898 John Gerritse dragged the cannon above the tide line with his team of horses. James Austin, believed to have been the postmaster, helped. Paul Bantel mounted the cannon in cement on Rudolph Kissling's property, where it remained for twenty years—thus was named the beach. Some controversy exists as to when the townspeople started calling their settlement Cannon Beach from the earlier established "Ecola," but in 1922, because of confusion over two post offices in Oregon named "Ecola," the beach resort's post office was changed to Cannon Beach. Long after the name of the town changed, the famous cannon was moved to its present site on the Oregon Coast Highway. It was dedicated on July 18, 1956.

As with other beaches that are long, broad and flat, Cannon Beach ranks high as a producer of glass fishing floats, bottles, light bulbs and other easily tossed about items.

There are several short beaches south of Cannon Beach to which access is gained either by car or trail. Hug Point State Park (picnicking—day use only), is one such area. Recalling that the beaches of Oregon are part of the state highway system, in the early days a ledge was chiseled and blasted away from the seaward side of the point to form a road. One can walk on this narrow shelf at low tide but the way is slippery. All of the beaches in this area are great glass float collectors and

(Above, left) Wheelbarrows for camping gear at Oswald West State Park. (right) Russian float found at Manzanita. (below) Manzanita beach.

sea animals cling to the rocks in abundance.

Probably the most quiet (and serene) public campground on the Northwest Coast is at Oswald West State Park (camping summer only—reservations). It is quiet because there are no campsites for motorized units—tents only. Access to the tent sites from the parking area is by *wheelbarrows* which may be borrowed from the park office to carry gear to the sites. Offshore rocks and a limited beach control the number of floats.

The wide beach at Nehalem Spit south of the town of Manzanita is another great collector of fishing floats. Consider camping at Nehalem Bay State Park (camping in summer only — reservations). Although few Soviet iron floats have been reported on any Northwest Coast beach in recent years, one of the eight-inch diameter, five pound rusty balls was picked up here in March 1977. The night before this find had been wild with a combination of high tide and a west wind.

The Manhattan Beach-Rockaway portion of the north coast — five miles of sand — has traditionally been an area where glass floats are found. In past years, large roller type floats have been picked up along here. There is a county park with trailer hookups at Barview (open all year) within walking distance of the beach near the north jetty.

The Bayocean Peninsula (Tillamook Spit) was for decades one of the better beaches for looking for wave tossed treasures. However, when the spit was broken and ripped apart (a mile wide) during the November 1952 storm, what was left of the beach went under water.

For at least three decades the once broad flat beach at Bayocean had been eaten away by erosion. Many fine homes along the seafront, as well as those high on dunes, slipped from their foundations, slid down the sand dunes and smashed on the beach below. A three story hotel was lost along with a natatorium which had an indoor swimming pool 160 feet long. During World War II, the Coast Guard rented one of the palatial houses for a Beach Patrol headquarters. The

Margie with Russian iron floats. Each float weighs between four and five pounds. Is about eight inches in diameter.

guardsmen tethered their war dogs in the remains of the hotel, which at that time was slowly coming apart and falling into the sea 140 feet below its perch on top of a sand dune.

In 1977 the beach at Bayocean is available only at low tide but what beachcombing! While researching for the book, *What Happened at Bayocean—Is Salishan Next?,* the authors spent a lot of time at Bayocean looking for evidence that there had, indeed, once been a town there. Found were large sections of concrete pavement with egg size rocks; sections of rail from the famous Bayocean Railroad; parts from a wood burning kitchen stove; a once porcelain but now rusty bath tub; a section of a well casing that had once been driven down through the 140 foot high sand dune to fresh water — the pipe (still standing) now nearly one-quarter mile at sea can be seen at low tide!

In March 1977 a key tag from rental units in Tent City at Bayocean was found by Bill and Marlene Springs of Tillamook.

Glass floats still land at Bayocean but because of almost no beach for long lengths of the seafront, most are carried right back out to sea. But some of the largest agates can be found here. Access to the seafront is by the Corps of Engineers' breakwater completed in 1956. Cars and campers can park in the lot provided (day use only). The lot is approximately where the main business corner of the town was. The walk to the beach is short, over Holland beach grass planted to

Bill McKeen found this extra large float at Netarts Bay.

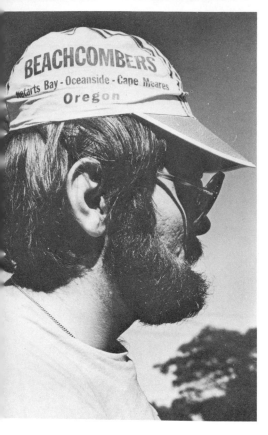

Beachcombers Festivals each spring draw thousands of "vicarious beachcombers." *See:* Chapter 21. (below) Even the family dog is a beachcomber!

control wind erosion.

It may be noted that the first street back from the water front at Cape Meares is "Third Street." First and Second Streets, and several buildings, fell into the sea as a part of the over-all erosion problems of the area.

The short beaches in the Oceanside and Netarts areas are high glass float producers. The local people take every opportunity to enjoy these beaches — and fetch in the floats — many of which are almost in some of their front yards.

The Netarts-Oceanside-Cape Meares Beachcombers Fair (each March), is probably the oldest of such get togethers anywhere along the Northwest Coast.

Maxwell Point is at the north end of Oceanside, and is the access route to Short Beach. At low tide one might walk around the point where communities of intertidal animals can be observed and photographed. Just above the high tide line there is a tunnel through the point to Short Beach.

Netarts Spit is seldom beachcombed because of its inaccessibility. Unless one has a good boat and access to the water for crossing at the mouth of Netarts Bay, the only way to the spit is the walk from Cape Lookout State Park (Camping all year — reservations in summer). The walk is long and hard, as much as eleven miles round trip, and requires advance preparation. These plans would include hiking boots, drinking water, lunch, and probably an established camp in the state park to relax in upon return.

Hiking on the beach is fun but it can be a task on stormy or windy days. The prevailing wind is southerly therefore to walk to the north is easy. But the trip back, "into the teeth of the bloomin' gale," can be wearysome and downright hard if one is lugging a load of treasures picked up along the way.

The beach in front of Boy Scout Camp Meriweather, immediately south of Cape Lookout, is another of the better beaches for finding glass floats. Winter storms bring them in and only special weekend troops of Scouts use the camp in the off season. One Scout, several seasons back, wanted to walk the beach at night so he and a buddy set out. In less than one hour they struggled back to their tent burdened with half-a-dozen ten-inch floats which they said had been taken within a few feet of each other right in front of the camp. The authors' ten-inch float is from this midnight beachwalk. Incidentally, the Scout Camp is closed to public access to the beach.

Rocks are plentiful on parts of this beach. One March morning the authors located remains of a large float—one that had broken on the rocks. The pieces were gathered and later that day displayed at the nearby Beachcombers Fair. A quickly lettered sign placed alongside the heap of broken glass read, "A float that didn't make it."

The long, flat, beach continues south from Cape Lookout for some miles past Sand Lake and Terra Del Mar to Cape Kiwanda, where beachcombing is seriously followed by many of the local people. When motor vehicles are permitted on the beach, the chances of finding floats before a commercial collector gets to them are somewhat limited. Yet there are dozens of instances where the jeep drivers, who appear to exceed the speed limit, do not concentrate on finding floats. Unless the floats are high and dry and all alone on the sand, these drivers often miss many. The fellow and girl who picked up the "Rusty Russian" float at Manzanita did so from a small heap of seaweed and ocean foam. There were vehicle tracks within feet of the spot where the float was retrieved.

About one mile southwest of Cape Kiwanda is another monolith also named Haystack Rock. At 327 feet high it is considerably taller than Haystack Rock on Cannon Beach. The pinnacle is also a sanctuary for birds thus trespassing is prohibited.

The county park on Whalen Island (camping—open all year), five miles north of Pacific City is comfortable and quiet.

The beach and tide at Pacific City is unique for here is where fishing dorries are launched directly into the ocean from trailers. Because of the heavy traffic on the beach in the boat launching area, little beachcombing is carried out. Further south, including Nestucca Spit, the chances for finding trophies are much better.

The area around Neskowin has always been a favorite for beachcombers. So favorite, that summer homes and a large motel with its vacation-time crowds covers the beach as a crowd of sandpipers.

The Northwest Coast is a rugged, spectacular place to visit, to study, and to beachcomb. Yet there are some dangers involved in addition to getting the car

Unstable driftwood on Siletz (Salishan) Spit. Inn at Spanish Head, Lincoln City, center, rear.

stuck in the sand or being isolated in a cove on an incoming tide. The view from Cascade Head is exciting and it is a popular place to go. *But stay away from the edge of the cliff!* All too frequently newspaper headlines are made when somebody falls off.

The areas of Lincoln City and Siletz (Salishan) Spit a few miles south, have been the scenes of continuing coastal erosion for years. Managers of resort type motels at Lincoln City sometimes are awakened in the middle of a stormy night with reports of huge drift logs that have been hurled by King Neptune through windows, or breakers that have crashed against the building, pushed in the glass and flooded rooms. A restaurant manager whose place overhangs the beach had to send diners to the hospital for glass cuts during one storm—the breakers had roared extra high and had shattered his plate glass windows.

From a point just north of Lincoln City and for a distance to the south, the Chamber of Commerce coined the phrase, "Twenty Miracle Miles." In this length of coastline there are frequent beach accesses, excellent beachcombing, and lots of walkers on the beach. Devil's Lake State Park (camping—summer only), is near the center of town just off the Oregon Coast Highway. Be alert to the "No Overnight Parking" signs at D River State Wayside which faces the beach at the D River Bridge.

The D River is reported to be the world's shortest river—only 440 feet long. During some severe winter storms, King Neptune throws driftwood the size of telephone poles over the seaward side of the D River bridge and onto the Oregon Coast Highway.

Siletz (Salishan) Spit is an area for hardy beachcombers who usually hit the beach early and stay all day. The Salishan Properties operates a locked (key card) gate to the palatial homes on the spit. Public access to this public beach is from Gleneden Beach State Park (picnicking—day use only). Of course the best beachcombing is on sloppy days so warm watertight clothing, boots, drinking water and a pocket lunch are all indicated. The hike of several miles to the north end of the spit can be rewarding for the spit is a haven for glass floats and all sizes of driftwood.

A word of caution seems advisable for stormy days and high tides. The driftwood is very unstable and moves easily under foot. Breakers, at times, cover the entire beach. In January 1973, a two story house under construction tumbled to the beach when King Neptune decided he wanted his sand back. Breakers had crashed and pounded one after another at the base of the dune until the dune came apart and the house fell over the edge to the beach about twenty feet below. (Recollections of Bayocean some twenty years earlier!) The following spring, thousands of yards of rock was hauled and dumped on the sand in front of many homes—and the next winter King Neptune winked at man's folly and promptly collapsed many of the rows of rocks. A representative of the Oregon State Department of Geology and Mineral Industries who did investigations on Siletz Spit was quoted, "As a geologist I wouldn't build a house there."

Tides bring in huge deposits of driftwood to Siletz Spit and on the next tide just as many logs may wash right back out to sea. The spit has always been a great place to look for glass fishing floats. And sometimes the sea parks other objects on the beach too.

The new ferro-concrete schooner *Marjean* was lost near the end of the spit on December 31, 1972, while on its maiden shakedown cruise. Heavy seas forced the helpless 48-feet long yacht onto the beach after the engine failed. The occupants jumped off and walked to a house for help.

Within days King Neptune threw large logs at the stricken vessel which caused severe damage. In addition, the hull had cracked under the hammering of

Marjean.

Beachcombers might find traces of *Marjean* at low tide if King Neptune has disturbed the sand a little on the last high.

the sea and sand had been sluiced away from the hull with each receding wave. To stop this erosion of the beach a bull dozer was summoned. The 'dozer dug a pit, smashed the hull, and the remains of the schooner whose owner had envisioned an around-the-world cruise, were shoved into the hole and covered with sand. This was reported to have been a $100,000 loss. At times, depending on wave action, portions of the concrete hull and some of the three-sixteenths-inch diameter iron reinforcing rods can be seen protruding from the beach.

Fogarty Creek State Park (picnicking—day use only) has a foot tunnel running under the Oregon Coast Highway for easier access to the flat beach. Nearby residents keep the sandy beach picked clean of collectables. Fogarty Park is a favorite for summer picnickers. The beach is relatively small, very flat, is bisected by a creek, and children play on exposed rocks and build castles near them at low tide. An area on both sides of the creek contains populations of intertidal animals which are collectable by permit only.

The sandy and flat beach in front of Beverly Beach State Park (camping all year—reservation in summer) is a high production area for glass floats. This good hunting ground continues south to the end of Moolack Beach near Yaquina Head where there is a lighthouse.

We have seen that the town of Cannon Beach was named for a cannon washed ashore following the wreck of a ship. And from another ship's fitting comes the name for Boiler Bay.

Fogerty Beach State Park. High tides usually surround or cover all rocks shown.

Boiler Bay gets its name from boiler from ship *J. Marhoffer.* Area abounds with intertidal life.

On May 18, 1910, the little coastal steamer *J. Marhoffer* was wrecked and the boiler came to rest close inshore among rocks. The old boiler remains to this day and can be seen and walked out to at low tide. The trail to the boiler, and intertidal animal communities, is steep and in wet weather it is muddy and slippery.

For the beachcomber with a camera who wants to make color photos which are different, aim for the sponges at Shell Cove. Take Shell Cove Road near the south end of the City of Depoe Bay, and drive west then south paralleling the shore. The bedrock that juts into the sea forms a ledge where there are numerous tide pools. A large spray zone is indicative of the great force the breakers expend on the rocks. The channel walls are covered with populations of sponge in yellow, red, green and purple—a photographer's delight!

At Yaquina Head there are two areas suitable for beachcombing. For access to the north side, leave the Oregon Coast Highway at Shell Road at the north end of Agate Beach, turn west past Fossil Street and proceed to the end of the street. A poor trail goes down to the sandy beach. Because of the angle of the landform, a northwesterly wind will drive much flotsam and jetsam into the shore here. At the south end of the beach are intertidal colonies of sponges and other protected sea life.

The south side beach is reached from Lighthouse Road in the town of Agate Beach. The road eventually dead ends at the Yaquina Head Lighthouse. The poorly marked, and poor quality trail to south side beach is in the vicinity of a gravel quarry. The shelf areas in the rock outcroppings contain extensive fields of purple sea urchins and large populations of starfish, barnacles and mussels.

One can walk south along the beach directly to Agate Beach (the name of the town as well as the name for a beach). Agate Beach Wayside has a large parking area for day use. It has been said that one can pick up agates at any time of the year and in any weather at Agate Beach. The area has been so popular for its agates and summer homes—now occupied year around—that a post office, Agate

Beach, Oregon, has been operating there since 1912.

South Beach State Park (camping summer only—reservations) is just south of the bridge over Yaquina Bay. The park can be a base for operations that could last several days. This is a relatively new state park and much of the loose sand still drifts freely. The beach just beyond the high dune is long, relatively flat and produces a wide variety of driftwood and glass floats. From the camp one can drive the short distance to Oregon State University's Marine Science Center. Permits for taking intertidal animals, in areas where permits are required, can be obtained from the Marine Region of the Oregon Fish and Wildlife Commission at the Marine Science Center.

The Center is open to the public year around. There are exhibits, many aquariums, a book counter, and guides for groups. Between late May and early September there are workshops (two days—fee), talks, films and nature walks all open to the public and mostly free. These events are part of the SEATAUQUA (see-TALK-wa), a cooperative program sponsored by Oregon State University Summer Term Office; the University Extension Service; School of Oceanography; Marine Science Center; Sea Grant College Program and other contributors from OSU's Corvallis campus.

The coast along the central part of Oregon is generally narrow, accumulates driftwood but few glass floats. There are some exceptions however, and Seal Rock State Park (picnicking—day use only) is one of them. From the park a massive headland points in a southwesterly direction off shore from which are numerous rocks and reefs. The rocks are frequently covered with seals and sea lions. A sandy beach over one hundred yards in length becomes a resting place for glass floats that have been tossed over the offshore reef by winter storms.

Some beachcombers are fortunate in obtaining a campsite at Beachside State Park (camping in summer—reservations), facing the ocean and beautiful sunsets.

Carl G. Washburne State Park (camping—summer only), a few miles south of Beachside, is across the highway, behind a dune and is protected by trees. It is quiet. Often space can be found here (no reservations) when Beachside is full.

From Washburne to Eel Creek U.S. Forest Service camp, fifteen miles north of North Bend, there are eleven camps with overnight facilities.

Serious beachcombers may be able to drive by most roadside attractions, but with kids along the sudden appearance of signs on a narrow, cliff-side highway announcing, "Sea Lion Caves," will bring them instantly alive. (Fee attraction—open all year.) The cave is said to be the only *mainland* sea lion home in the world. A great grotto was carved in the rocks thousands of years ago and here herds of sea lions make their home. In addition, Cormorant, Tufted Puffin and Pigeon

Southbound travelers on U.S. Highway 101 (Oregon Coast Highway) near Cape Perpetua, a few miles south of Waldport find frequent turnouts to stop in to enjoy the view. Many campgrounds in immediate area.

Intertidal life is protected along Northwest Coast. For preserving starfish, *see:* Appendix E.

Guillemot as well as Herring Sea Gulls nest in the cave and on nearby cliffs. During summer, the weather can be quite comfortable but one may become chilly in the caves. (Too, sea lions have not yet oriented themselves to the use of deodorants!)

One of the major highways from Interstate Freeway I-5 crosses the Coast Range and terminates at the coast in this area. Jesse M. Honeyman Memorial State Park (camping all year—reservations in summer) is just south of Florence where Highway 126 delivers beachcombers to the coast from Eugene.

Heceta (he-SEE-tuh) Beach is a graceful area which can be reached from the

Public swimming with locker room is within Honeyman State Park.

Oregon Coast Highway. The small beach is good for general beachcombing but here again visitors need be mindful of the tide schedules, wind speed and direction, and be on the beach before the year around residents get to the glass floats first.

The wide sandy beach of the Oregon Dunes Recreation Area which includes Siuslaw (sseye-YOO-slaw) Spit, has numerous access points all south of Florence.

Oregon Dunes National Recreation Area, Oregon Coast.

There is uninterrupted beach extending about twenty miles south to Winchester Bay. Across the Umpqua (UHMP-kwaw) River the dunes continue for another twenty miles. Except for being cut by the Umpqua River, these two beaches are the longest on the Northwest Coast. (The Long Beach Peninsula on the Washington Coast is about twenty eight *continuous* miles long.)

The Oregon Dunes are administered by the Siuslaw National Forest and they are for everyone to enjoy. The total dune area is about fifty miles long and extends inland from the ocean front between one and three miles. Pieces of sandblasted wood, usually bleached gray, gnarled, and prized by beachcombers, can be found here. These sand blasted pieces are frequently more valued than general driftwood. Japanese glass fishing floats are commonly found in *summer* but not along the beach. Authorities suggest beachcombers look near the base of the foredune—the line of dunes paralleling the ocean—where wind uncovers floats deposited during the winter which were overlooked earlier in the year.

Driftwood, parts from old shipwrecks, bottles, light bulbs, a plethora of plastic junque, much kelp—some very white and dry—agates and seashells can be found in these miles of beach.

Visiting the Oregon Dunes Recreation Area for serious beachcombing requires advance preparation. Have available good shoes or boots, bathing suits and hats for the hot weather; or rain gear for the sloppy days, drinking water and picnic lunches. The Oregon Dunes offer endless opportunities for photography.

Honeyman Memorial State Park can be an excellent base for beachcombing sessions along the north end of the Oregon Dunes Recreation Area.

There is a county camp ground at Windy Cove, Winchester Bay (open all year), as well as Umpqua Lighthouse State Park (camping in summer only—reservations), from which trips along the coast south of the Umpqua River can be

47

(Top) High tide at Bullard's Beach, Bullard's Beach State Park, January 1977 during heavy rain. Camera on jetty facing north. December 1977 tides washed out beach, damaged parking lot, left huge tangle of heavy driftwood. By late March 1978, beach, adjacent to jetty, was under water at high tide. (left) Abandoned Lighthouse on North Jetty, mouth of Coquille River. Access from Bullard's Beach State Park. Can be photographed from N. Jetty (as shown) or from S. Jetty in City of Bandon.

staged. It is interesting to recall that all of these beaches were watched by the Coast Guardsman, many with war dogs, and some mounted, during the second world war. In what is now the Oregon Dunes Recreation Area, there were Beach Patrol Units stationed at Siuslaw River, Siltcoos, Umpqua River and Saunders Lake.

Tugman State Park (camping—summer only) is just off Highway 101 about mid-way between Winchester Bay and the City of North Bend. From the north, getting out to the spit west of North Bend is possible by taking the off ramp to the west after seeming to enter the long narrow approach to the tall bridge over Coos Bay. Approaching from the south while high on the bridge, one can see the off ramp on pilings and a fill to the *left* which bisects the highway in the middle of the bay. This ramp leads to some access roads to the beach and to a Forest Service campground at Horsfall Lake. In fact, there are several Forest Service camps along highway 101 throughout the nearly fifty mile length of the dunes.

SOUTH OREGON COAST

The character of the coast south of Coos Bay is completely different than we have observed to the north. Where sandy beaches dominate the shoreline in the north portion of Oregon, these give way to unique rock formations, small sandy coves, exquisite opportunities for creative photography, but far fewer camp grounds. The South Coast is not as traveled therefore it is not as noisy and confused with roadside eateries and other establishments. The Oregon Coast Highway winds around hills, climbs some steep capes and drivers need to watch for open-range sheep which commonly wander onto the highway.

Arago Lighthouse—most picturesque—is two miles south of Charleston. Bastendorf Beach County Campground (open all year) is nearby. Access to the view point of Arago is by a narrow paved road but a locked gate on the bridge at the small parking lot bars entrance to the Coast Guard property. Access to the

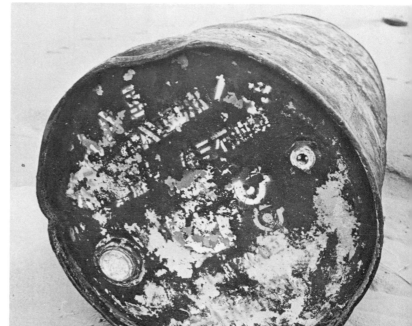

A great treasure for a beachcomber, but too big and too heavy for most to carry away.

There are dozens of short beaches along the Oregon coast, particularly in the south. At right, the short beach at Hug Point State Park.

beach is very poor. The intertidal (permit) area consists of some sizeable pools where purple sea urchins and red sea cucumbers can be seen in addition to other common animals. Occasionally glass fishing floats are present after a severe storm.

Sunset Bay is a snug little cove less than one-half mile south of the lighthouse. Sunset Bay State Park (camping in summer only—reservations), with an excellent picnic area is here. The bay has a sandy beach with sheer cliffs and flat shelf areas at each end. Channels of varying depths have been cut through the rocks by *aeons* of years of pounding breakers. These channels are potentially dangerous during incoming tides.

The photographic possibilities are endless because of the various angles of the sun's reflection on the bay and rocks, particularly at the end of the day.

It should be pointed out the Arago Lighthouse is not on Cape Arago—the cape being several miles to the south. The intertidal areas are to the north and south of the cape. North Cove is the largest. It is easily accessible and there is ample parking. The immense intertidal area extends to Shell Island and beyond on lower tides. There is a sandy beach. Offshore, large herds of seals and sea lions can be seen, heard (and sometimes smelled!).

There is a Middle Cove where a well constructed trail leads to the small beach and intertidal area.

Although the trail to the beach at South Cove is steep, walkers will be rewarded by viewing beds of bull kelp, which because of its size quiets subtidal wave action. South Cove is noted for sea urchins, star fish, chitons and crab.

Whiskey Run Beach is about mid-way between Coos Bay and Bandon and is

"After the Storm," an oil painting by Emma Blankinship. (bottom) Beachcombed treasures displayed in restaurant window at Winchester Bay.

accessible from a secondary road off the Oregon Coast Highway. There is very limited parking for cars and small campers. *(Trailers should probably be dropped at Bullard's Beach State Park. Recreational Vehicles may not be able to turn around especially if there are automobiles already there.)*

Gold dust can still be obtained from Whiskey Run Creek near the beach. It was on this beach that the authors found their first Japanese glass float. I was a little larger than a golf ball! The beach is long, quite shallow, and subject to pounding breakers during severe storms.

The beach at Bullard's Beach State Park (camping all year—reservations in

summer) is long, reasonably wide and flat, and is a good place to look for driftwood and floats in season. Breakers crash violently on the beach during winter and early spring storms, and one can sit in a car and watch these masses of exploding energy for hours.

South of the Coquille River and west of Bandon is a series of short beaches all noted for fishing float production. One day the authors found a fifty-five-gallon oil drum with Japanese markings. The drum was just too large and too heavy to haul home! There is plenty of driftwood here but mainly upstream about fifty yards from the mouth of a creek. The rocks forming intertidal pools are fairly well covered with orange and purple star fish and anenomes.

West of Langlois, the beachcombing is excellent on the narrow sandy stretches, but permission must be obtained from private land holders to get to the shoreline.

The westernmost *point* in Oregon, Cape Blanco, is about ten miles north of Port Orford. The Coast Guard lighthouse and Cape Blanco State Park (camping — summer only) are six miles west of the Oregon Coast Highway on a paved road. (There is a large private camp ground, open all year, at the intersection of the Oregon Coast Highway and the road to the cape.) The beach on the north side of the cape has been noted for bottles and fishing floats, while the south beach is the driftwood cache. Access to the north area is by unimproved trails (sheep paths) down a football field-length steep hill just before reaching the Coast Guard property. All of the north beach area is active with intertidal life extending fifty to one hundred yards offshore. The beach is sandy and windy. If one arrives at lunch time, eat in the car before descending the hill since this combination of sand and wind almost guarantees that sand will get into the peanut butter.

Visiting the Coast Guard Station by the public is limited to posted hours. At times, tours of the now automatically operated light house are offered. While there are trails down the cliff at the west end of the cape to intertidal areas, these trails are unsafe. There is a short, narrow, tunnel connecting the north and west ends of the cape, but this is accessible only at low tide. Tide pools and crevices in the rocks are frequent and the cliffs down to the sea are mostly perpendicular. The Coast Guard dissuades people from going down the dangerous west end trails for there is great risk of being trapped by incoming tides. Tidal action is severe and the wind

Lighthouse at Cape Blanco (*See*: Pg. 177)

blows most of the time.

Within sight of the lighthouse, the 4,900-ton tanker *J. A. Chanslor* was wrecked on the jagged rocks off Cape Blanco during a storm in December 1919. Thirty-six of the thirty-nine men on board were lost after all were swept off the ship by titanic-size breakers. It is doubtful that a cry for help would be heard above the howling wind by Coast Guardsmen inside their station, nearly one hundred yards back from the top of the 225-foot high cliff.

At Battle Rock State Wayside (picnicking, view - day use only) within the City of Port Orford, is parking space close to Battle Rock and the beach.

After visitors have read the paragraph about Battle Rock on the roadside marker, it is easy to envision the battle that took place on the rock. Nine men finally escaped from the rock following attacks by over two hundred Indians on the day of the first attempt to found the town in 1851. In following years, sailing ships seeking shelter from King Neptune's fury, anchored in the bay immediately south of Battle Rock.

(Above) Battle Rock at Port Orford as viewed from below parking area at Battle Rock State Wayside. Humbug Mountain in left rear. (right) Facing south from within "cave" in Battle rock.

It is easy to scramble over the driftwood to Battle Rock without getting wet feet, even at most high tides for the driftwood deposit is quite thick. The beach is relatively steep. Although glass floats have been reported, these finds are infrequent here for visitors, as the locals keep a pretty sharp eye out for them.

Intertidal animals have been observed by the writers at the water line on the north side of Battle Rock and sometimes within the short narrow tunnel through the rock. Access to the short tunnel is at low tide.

Rocky Point is about three miles south of Port Orford and just inside Humbug Mountain State Park (camping—summer only). From a dirt road with limited parking, the beach is about one hundred yards away. This beach has a gentle slope with many boulders two feet or less in size scattered around. Offshore reefs onto which glass floats crash and break, and kelp beds which trap floats, modify wave action here. Intact floats have not often been reported here but broken glass, mostly of the common aqua (coke bottle) float color, is sometimes seen. (Wear Shoes!)

The Humbug Mountain State Park intertidal area and beach, is reached from a trail at the west end of the camp ground. The rocky area is made up of several cliffs jutting from the mainland. There are many boulders on the sand. The beach is exposed to very heavy winter surf (when the campground is closed) and driftwood, floats and general flotsam and jetsam come in—then frequently wash back out to sea on the next wave or tide.

There are four Safety Rest Areas along the Oregon Coast Highway, at this writing, and all are within about sixty miles of the Oregon—California border. The infrequency of parks and commercial facilities appears to be the reason for this. The most northerly of these Rest Areas is at Ophir, about ten miles north of Gold Beach. Tents may not be pitched in Safety Rest Areas however motor vehicles

Arizona Beach and campground.

are permitted to "rest" (occupied or unattended) for up to eighteen hours in any twenty-four hour period. The beach to the north and south of Ophir is open to the wildest of winter storms and good beachcombing is assured. Directly below the parking area (near the rest rooms) there is a long gravel bed midway between the low and high tide lines which is rich with agates.

Arizona Beach is about three miles north of Ophir where there is a large private camp ground open all year. One must pass through the grounds for access to the beach. Campers and trailers can use hookups on a ledge just a few feet above the beach but tenters will be comfortable in the bushy area back from the shore line and away from the brisk winds. (In summer, blackberries the size of one's thumb can be found in the tent area.)

Arizona beach is flat and sandy. Mussel Creek empties into the ocean through the middle of the 300-yard long beach. On each side of the creek are intertidal pools with mussel colonies, starfish and sea cucumbers. Possibilities for closeup color photography are endless here.

A few hundred yards south of Arizona Beach is a tourist (fee) attraction, The Prehistoric Gardens. As mentioned earlier, many beachcombing adults can drive right by a roadside attraction with hardly any notice. But with children along—that may be difficult.

Prehistoric Gardens has been painstakenly hand built in a secluded area of big trees and moss along Fromm Creek in a rain forest on the west side of the Oregon Coast Highway. This is one of the most unusual attractions in the world. Prehistoric Gardens contains life-size replicas of dinosaurs placed among primitive plants (all identified) that grow profusely in this small sheltered valley.

Ernie Nelson purchased the property in the early 1950's. Since then he has developed it to where it has become the largest private collection of prehistoric animal likenesses set in natural surroundings anywhere. The displays are scientifically correct with sizes and shapes based on measurements of mounted

Life-size dinosaurs are on display at Prehistoric Gardens south of Port Orford.

skeletons displayed in museums. Nelson creates these exhibits in his shop on the property.

The displays are constructed by modeling cement mortar over frames of steel and metal lath. The giant bird, *Diatryma* required 2,335 concrete feathers and was nearly two years in construction.

The Prehistoric Gardens is open from 8 a.m. until dusk all year and caters to children and adults alike. Patrons can spend as much time as they like in the Gardens. Kids have only one speed — wide open — as they let off steam racing along the fenced trails. Adults spend the longest time studying details (from descriptive display boards) of the prehistoric monsters. Photographic possibilities are unlimited. A wide-angle lens is an advantage.

Those seeking campsites along the South Coast have already observed that such facilities are considerably farther apart than along the North Coast. Motels and trailer courts are not as frequent in the south either. There are some deluxe resort type accommodations. Local Chambers of Commerce have the information and libraries frequently have national guides listing these. Huntly Park, a wilderness type camp site (open all year) is available as a public service by a lumber company on the south bank of the Rogue River. The camp is a few miles upstream from the south end of the bridge at Gold Beach.

Samuel Boardman State Park is a narrow, spectacular area along the southern Oregon coast for about eleven miles. It includes one of the most rugged and picturesque sections of the Oregon coast. The park has several driveways from the Oregon Coast Highway which end at beaches, coves, view points and intertidal

Rugged South Oregon coast. (below) Lone Ranch Beach Safety Rest Area.

areas. Some picnic tables are available. There are trails from parking areas. From the view points one sees spectacular vistas of vertical cliffs plunging into the sea, massive off-shore rocks and crashing surf. Watch for signs indicating which driveways will *NOT* accommodate trailers or large campers. The narrow park zone is bordered by private land therefore access is only on the driveways provided by the state. The few beaches are shallow and are noted for their lack of production of glass floats and driftwood however intertidal life abounds. Although driftwood is often found in small protected areas, the waves that might leave the wood usually take the slippery glass floats right back into the sea.

About seven miles north of Brookings the highway crosses Thomas Creek Bridge where there is a Safety Rest Area. At 345 feet this is the highest bridge in Oregon. Driftwood piles up in the petite cove where Thomas Creek empties into the ocean. Except for the most hardy, the mouth of the creek is inaccessible

There is good beachcombing at the mouth of the Pistol River with parking at Pistol River State Park (picnicking—day use only). At this river outlet the coastline is flat for short distances. Fog often comes rolling in here, wind can be brisk and large RV's and cars with trailers are cautioned to be wary of wind gusts.

Lone Ranch Beach Safety Rest Area at the base of Cape Ferrelo is a part of Boardman State Park. The driveway down to the parking lot is quite steep—easy

Harris Beach State Park.
Beach and intertidal area.

to get down with a trailer but on the way back up many experience tenseness on trying to get onto the highway again. An arterial STOP on the severe grade must be made before entering the highway. The authors do not recommend taking a trailer, or a car with a slipping clutch to Lone Ranch Beach Safety Rest Area.

Beachcombers will find excellent trails for easy access to the beach from the parking lot. The sandy beach has many rocks varying in size from less than one foot to small cliffs. Tide pools are few, but numerous rocky overhangs and caves provide protection from pounding waves for intertidal animals. But the small beach area does not have much chance of retaining many glass floats. Due to the limited accessibility and fewer visitors in this part of the Oregon Coast the flora and fauna are relatively undisturbed.

Harris Beach State Park (camping all year — reservations in summer) is at the north city limits of Brookings. There are three main areas of the park to consider.

North Harris Beach is reached from the north end of the parking area beyond the rest rooms at the bottom of the cliff. The beach is sandy, sloping, about one hundred yards long, then merges with a rocky point. This point is partially broken by erosion. There are isolated rocks. Extending north are additional rocky projections between which are sandy coves. These alternating beaches and rocks eventually merge into Lone Ranch Beach.

Beachcombers who anticipate the approximately six mile walk (round trip) between Harris Beach and Lone Ranch Beach, will want to protect their feet with heavy boots as well as being aware of incoming tides. Many of the sandy coves, which contain an abundance of beached material, are reached only at low tide because of the limited access from the highway — which does not parallel the sea front. Carry drinking water, camera, dependable watch and a tide chart. (Beachcombers should acquaint themselves with time difference computations which are required to properly read a tide chart.) Go in pairs or groups. The area closes at sundown. Hiking on the low tide-exposed rocks and in the sandy coves at night is unsafe. To camp on a secluded beach that appears to be in a sheltered cove might prove to have been a deadly decision when the tide comes in.

The main Harris Beach has a large intertidal animal population directly west of the campgrounds. A massive rock juts southward into the sea. Waves surge through a small tunnel in the rock and flood the boulder fields landward. As one goes south this boulder field is replaced by a cliff. Other scatterings of boulders are interrupted by small stretches of beaches. Continuing south are many steep cliffs and outcroppings with several short sandy coves between. The area is rugged and beautiful.

ASTORIA TIDE TABLES

CORRECTION TABLE
ASTORIA DISTRICT

To correct the TIME of HIGH or LOW tides for the points given below, add or subtract TIME from the ASTORIA District Tide Table. Also, add or subtract FEET to correct the HEIGHT of the HIGH TIDE.

OREGON COAST

	Time	Feet
Wedderburn, Rogue River	−1:45	−1.5
Port Orford	−1:50	−0.9
Bandon, Coquille River	−1:35	−1.3
Coos Bay Entrance	−1:25	−1.1
Empire, Coos Bay	−0:40	−1.5
Coos Bay (port) frly Marshf'd	0:00	−0.8
Umpqua River, Entrance	−1:20	−1.2
Gardiner	−0:25	−1.4
Siuslaw River Entrance	−1:15	−1.2
Waldport, Alsea Bay Entrance	−1:00	−0.5
Newport	−1:15	−0.2
Yaquina	−1:05	0.0
Toledo	−0:25	−0.1
Nestucca Bay Entrance	−0:55	−0.6
Garibaldi, Tillamook Bay	−1:10	−0.7
Nehalem River Entrance	−1:05	−0.4
Clatsop Beach	−1:00	−0.6

COLUMBIA RIVER

Entrance (North Jetty)	−1:00	−0.7
Ilwaco, Baker Bay, Wash.	−0:10	−0.5
Chinook, Baker Bay, Wash.	−0:30	−0.2
Point Adams, Ore.	−0:40	+0.1
Warrenton, Skipanon R., Ore.	−0:20	+0.2
Astoria, Young Bay, Ore.	−0:20	+0.4
Astoria (city) Ore.	−0:10	−0.2
Astoria (Tonque Point) Ore.	0:00	0.0

HIGH Tides ASTORIA District

DATE DAY		A. M. TIME	FT.	P. M. TIME	FT.
1	Wed	11:54	5.8	11:12	7.6
2	Thur	. . .	. .	12:42	6.4
3	Fri	0:12	8.0	1:18	7.1
4	Sat	1:06	8.2	1:54	7.7
5	SUN	1:54	8.3	2:30	8.2
6	Mon	2:42	8.2	3:12	8.6
7	Tues	3:30	7.8	3:48	8.9
8	Wed	4:24	7.3	4:24	8.9
9	Thur	5:18	6.6	5:06	8.8
10	Fri	6:18	6.0	6:00	8.4
11	Sat	7:30	5.5	7:00	7.9
12	SUN	8:48	5.3	8:06	7.4
13	Mon	10:06	5.5	9:24	7.2
14	Tues	11:12	5.8	10:36	7.2
15	Wed	12:00	6.3	11:36	7.3
16	Thur	. . .	. .	12:42	6.8
17	Fri	0:24	7.4	1:18	7.1
18	Sat	1:12	7.4	1:48	7.4
19	SUN	1:54	7.3	2:18	7.6
20	Mon	2:30	7.2	2:48	7.7
21	Tues	3:06	7.0	3:12	7.8
22	Wed	3:42	6.7	3:36	7.8
23	Thur	4:24	6.4	4:06	7.7
24	Fri	5:06	6.0	4:36	7.6
25	Sat	5:48	5.6	5:12	7.5
26	SUN	6:54	5.3	6:00	7.2
27	Mon	8:06	5.1	7:00	7.0
28	Tues	9:24	5.3	8:24	6.9
29	Wed	10:24	5.8	9:42	7.0
30	Thur	11:12	6.4	10:54	7.3

LOW Tides ASTORIA District

DATE DAY		A. M. TIME	FT.	P. M. TIME	FT.
1	Wed	5:24	−0.3	5:18	2.9
2	Thur	6:18	−0.8	6:18	2.3
3	Fri	7:00	−1.0	7:12	1.5
4	Sat	7:42	−1.1	8:00	0.7
5	SUN	8:24	−1.0	8:48	−0.1
6	Mon	9:00	−0.6	9:36	−0.5
7	Tues	9:42	−0.1	10:24	−1.0
8	Wed	10:18	0.6	11:12	−1.1
9	Thur	11:00	1.3	. . .	. .
10	Fri	0:06	−0.9	11:48	2.0
11	Sat	1:12	−0.7	12:48	2.6
12	SUN	2:18	−0.4	2:00	3.0
13	Mon	3:24	−0.2	3:24	3.1
14	Tues	4:36	−0.3	4:42	2.8
15	Wed	5:30	−0.4	5:42	2.4
16	Thur	6:24	−0.4	6:36	1.8
17	Fri	7:06	−0.4	7:24	1.3
18	Sat	7:42	−0.2	8:00	0.9
19	SUN	8:12	0.1	8:42	0.5
20	Mon	8:48	0.5	9:12	0.2
21	Tues	9:12	0.9	9:48	0.0
22	Wed	9:42	1.4	10:18	0.0
23	Thur	10:06	1.8	10:54	0.0
24	Fri	10:30	2.3	11:36	0.1
25	Sat	11:00	2.7	. . .	. .
26	SUN	0:30	0.2	11:42	3.0
27	Mon	1:30	0.3	12:48	3.4
28	Tues	2:36	0.3	2:24	3.4
29	Wed	3:42	0.1	3:48	3.1
30	Thur	4:42	−0.1	5:00	2.4

SAMPLE TIDE CHART

Tide charts are generally available from Chambers of Commerce and in most sporting goods and bait shops in towns fronting the ocean. Most tide charts are given free but some firms charge for them. Tide timing is a responsibility of the U.S. Department of Commerce, National Oceanic and Atmospheric Administration, which issues tide charts based on certain points along the coasts. Example here based on Astoria (Tongue Point) District. To correct a tide time for a given point away from the "base," add or subtract clock time as shown in "correction" instructions printed in every tide chart.

Along the South Oregon Coast. (inset) Intertidal areas within City of Brookings, facing northwest. (above) Mouth of Winchuck River from north bank.

Due to the large number of rocks and limited beaches, few glass balls are to be found along here. What few do come in are usually picked up by the locals during the crest of the tide.

Mill Beach is the southernmost part of the Harris Beach area. Drive toward the ocean on Center Street in downtown Brookings, then turn right at the plywood mill and stop next to a small ball park. An unimproved road leads to a bench above the beach where trails go down to the beach. For access to the north end of Mill Beach a drainage creek must be crossed between the plywood mill and the beach. During much of the year this area is muddy and not suitable for street shoes. To get to the south end of Mill Beach, take a trail from near the ball park past the sewage treatment plant. Mill Beach Cove is a halfmoon shaped area with steep headlands stretching into the ocean at each end. Near the base of those headlands are boulder fields and larger cliffs. The sandy beach is popular and well watched by nearby residents who appear as if they were radar-directed on the approach of beach bound glass floats.

Intertidal animals in the Harris Beach area can be taken by permit only. The population includes sponges, star fish, solitary corals and umbrella crabs.

Across the highway from the entrance to Harris Beach State Park is the Brookings Safety Rest Area

Loeb State Park (camping—summer only) is in a secluded grove of myrtle-wood (California laurel) trees eight miles up the east bank of the Chetco River. When the South Coast is foggy and cold, as often occurs during the summer

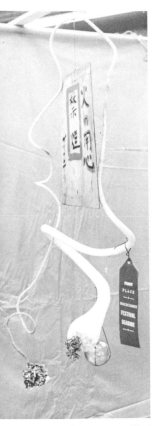

Kelp. (left) Dried, sunbleached kelp beachcombed from near mouth of Winchuck River was already shaped when found. Sign, which tells readers to stay away, gasoline, no smoking, was beachcombed between Cannon Beach and Arch Cape by authors. Sign is hand-painted on each side of this one-eighth-inch thick mahogany veneer. Mobile won ribbons at festivals in Seaside, Netarts, Bandon now retired in authors' home.

months, one will frequently encounter warm, dry weather at Loeb where dipping in the Chetco can often be very refreshing.

There are little or no beachcombing possibilities right at the mouth of the Chetco River. The beach is fairly steep and a trailer camping site is just a few feet from the sand. Crowds of people (mostly fishermen) take over the relatively small area. The river is confined between two jetties which account for the development of a brisk commercial and sports fishing interest here. But the Chetco was not always this way. When the first expedition on coastal survey arrived in August 1853, they found the river completely closed at the mouth by a heavy gravel bar.

One of the largest deposits of driftwood along the Oregon Coast is at the mouth of the Winchuck River just a few yards north of the Oregon—California line. There is a private campground on the north with access to an excellent beach. One can day-park in the public area on the north bank of the river and walk around the point to the beach where driftwood and dried kelp in all sizes and contortions abounds. A most prolific ribbon winning mobile at the beachcomber's festivals was made from a twisted, sun-dried kelp claimed from the north Winchuck Beach. The beach is steep and not productive of glass floats.

The sandy beach south of the river is flatter and there is much driftwood here also. Access to the south area is via a narrow road almost at the California line, then across the abandoned Crissey Airport to some unimproved roads which lead to the beach.

For many years the outlet of the Winchuck River resembled a large **S** and the major share of driftwood was on the north. About 1974 the sand built up at the

Picnicking and driftwood picking near mouth of Winchuck River.

mouth of the river to such an extent there was talk of bulldozing a new channel through the sand to the ocean. During the summer of 1975, beachcombers could walk across the former mouth of the river on dry sand, but in August 1976, the severe unseasonal rains caused the Winchuck River to rise. Within days, the swollen river burst through the sand. The swish of the backed up water washed years of dried driftwood out to sea to be later redistributed along the beach.

•   •   •

The Oregon Coast is scenic and both rugged and graceful. There is something along the coast to interest everyone whether it be camping, clam digging, agate hunting, driftwood searching, taking pictures, or eagerly beachcombing for elusive Japanese glass fishing floats. ☐

CHAPTER 5

BEACHCOMBER'S SANDTRAP

Having one's car get stuck in the sand can wreck a perfectly good day as well as the entire beachcombing and camping trip. Here are some suggestions for successful beach driving. The first is to observe the signs and make certain that vehicles are permitted on the particular stretch of beach where you are. Just because there is a driveway or ramp leading to a beach does not imply permission to drive on a beach. In Washington, *non-Indians are prohibited from all trespass on Reservation beaches. (See:* NOTES for CHAPTER 3.)

In Oregon, the best guide for determining which beaches motor vehicles can be operated upon is the official highway map issued by the Oregon State Transportation Commission. Along the left margin of this map is a color code showing percisely which beaches are open or closed to motor vehicles and when. In California, some beaches are privately owned and permission to trespass must be obtained in advance—sometimes for a fee.

Probably the most important trick to sand beach driving is to find a way to get *off* the beach. Some beach ramps are asphalt over which the sand has drifted. Others are rock fills. Some are constantly wet sand. Almost all of the ramps must be approached "straight on," or ninety degrees from the tide line, so the drive wheels will leave the firm sand and encounter the ramp at the same time. The shortcutting driver who approaches these ramps, some rather informal in construction, on an angle, frequently finds one drive wheel on the hard surface and the other caught in soft sand. As few cars are equipped with tools for digging out, the occupants of stuck cars are forced to search for a wrecker—and hopefully

Mere possession of four-wheel-drive truck with wide tires is no guarantee that such a vehicle can operate on beach sand.

they are able to locate one before the tide comes in!

Vehicles salvaged after being caught in the surf suffer extreme damage from salt as well as from sand. Some cars are washed out to sea, fill with sand from crashing breakers—sink—and are never seen again. Be aware that just because your camper is four-wheel-drive, this does not assume any ability of the vehicle to pull itself out of beach sand. There is nothing so pathetic as to watch a 4-wheeler dig itself deeper and deeper into the sand.

Quite often near the more populated beach ramps, there will be one or more 4-wheel-drive vehicles where volunteer "tow-artists" offer to show their skills by retrieving stuck cars and campers. These fellows work for the fun of it—no charge. But if one of these helpers damages a car while snaking it around, then who pays? The authors have been helped by the volunteer crops (with good results) and we were thankful for their availability. Unless the walk to a phone or to a wrecker station is too far, the best advice would be to hire a professional towing firm then stand back. With a commercial tow truck operator on the job, liability is his responsibility. When a credit card is used come settle up time later, quite often the receipt can be sent to an insurance company for reimbursement against towing insurance.

In an incident near the South Jetty at Fort Stevens State Park a few years ago, one of the volunteers had a loaded station wagon nearly out of the sand when the volunteer got stuck. A second weekend-4-wheel-drive cowboy came up, attached his winch to the rear of the station wagon to try to pull both units back to a little firmer ground. The three vehicles slowly started backward. In a few seconds they picked up speed, the rear bumper of the station wagon collapsed, so the wagon stopped dead in its tracks. The 4-wheeler in the front kept on backing and smashed the radiator of the station wagon. On seeing the damage, both volunteers roared off down the beach and out of sight.

If a commercial operator damages a car, he is probably well insured and a claim, although inconvenient, is just a matter of form. □

CHAPTER 6

VELELLA: THE PURPLE SAILFISH

Every storm to blow its way onto the shores of the Northwest Coast leaves debris of some kind along the beaches. Shells, frequently broken from snails, clams, crabs, as well as dying or dead sea animals come onto the sands just as do driftwood and fishing floats. Some years, particularly early in the spring, multitudes of by-the-wind-sailors, *Velella*, are deserted on the beaches by the wind-driven stormy sea.

Velella have triangular cellophane-like sails that reach for the wind that hurries them over the waves. It has been observed when *Velella* hit the beaches more likely than not glass fishing floats will be on the next tide!

The "fish," about two-inches by its longest dimension and purplish color, draws only a fraction of an inch of water and floats as a submarine with only its conning tower above water. But that "tower" is its sail. Contrary to older opinion, *Velella*, is not just a colony of specialized individuals, as is the stinging Portugese man-of-war, but a highly modified individual hydroid polyp that decided to live on top of the sea. Some hydroids, after hatching, sink to the bottom, grow like a stalk of corn and just stay there. But *Velella* developed a gas-filled float, stayed on top, then produced a very efficient, always erect, sail. They prefer the Temperate Zone of the Pacific Ocean. Beachcombers find remains of *Velella* and wonder how they got there.

Most of what we see and call *Velella* is, in reality, what is left of it. The little animals die and disintegrate after just a few days on the sand. Their skeletons by now bleached, aimlessly pile against driftwood and outcroppings of rock, or drift close to the sand whenever a whiff of air stirs.

The sail on a *Velella* is mounted on a diagonal to its length. If the Velella is pointed to the north, the sail will be noted to be in a northwest/southeast attitude

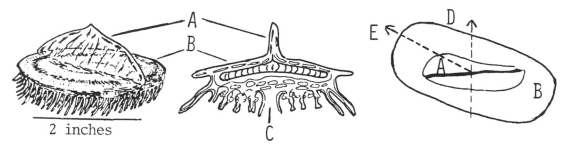

VELELLA (SAIL FISH)
A, SAIL B, FLOAT C, MOUTH D, WIND DIRECTION
E, FLOATING DIRECTION

on examples along the Northwest Coast beaches. It appears (but not yet proved), that two varieties of *Velella* exist side-by-side in the mid-Pacific Ocean. The second variety has its sail mounted on an opposite axis thus, "right-handed" and "left-handed" purple sail-fish. When blown before a moderate wind, *Velella* tacks at close to forty-five degrees when seen with its long axis at right angles to the wind. The presence of what we here term the "second variety," with sail on opposing angle, is found along the beaches of the Orient.

Velella along the Oregon and Washington coast tack to the left. Southerly winds blow these purplish sail-fish *away* from the shore — as southerlies also prohibit fishing floats from landing. On-shore west winds glide them right up onto the beaches. And glass floats with considerably more drag, generally follow just one high tide later. ☐

Pacific
Beach
State
Park.

CHAPTER 7

GLASS BALLS AND OCEANOGRAPHY

Beachcombing is a lot of fun and taking a very scientific approach to it seems to sap some of the pleasure from it. As one fellow remarked, "I'm a float hunter, not a float scientist." While too much science can boggle the brain, there are many who are interested in having a basic understanding of the forces which are involved in the beaching process.

We first acknowledge that fishing floats are lost from fishing operations somewhere in the vast North Pacific Ocean. Sometimes storms wash stocks of floats overboard from the fishing boats. Other times, floats, with nets attached, break loose from sea anchors in the fishing grounds and are left to drift. These floats can be of many national origins since many nations are currently fishing the North Pacific. Earlier, most of the fishing fleets were Japanese.

Interviews some years ago with crews returning to Japanese ports, established that many boats lost an average of fifty per cent of their fishing gear on every trip.

Regardless of where in the North Pacific Ocean a loss occurs, the non-sinkables, whether single glass balls or a mass entanglement of flotsam and jetsam, generally drift in a clockwise manner around the North Pacific Ocean. Pieces of floating matter will stay in the sea for years—decades—as vagabonds never touching land. But when the conditions are right, these floating trophies may land upon sandy beaches, or they could be smashed upon coastal rocks.

The mention has just been made of drifting "in a clockwise manner." The first question that arises is why the North Pacific Ocean flows in that direction? Although dissertations have been written about this, let us just say this direction has

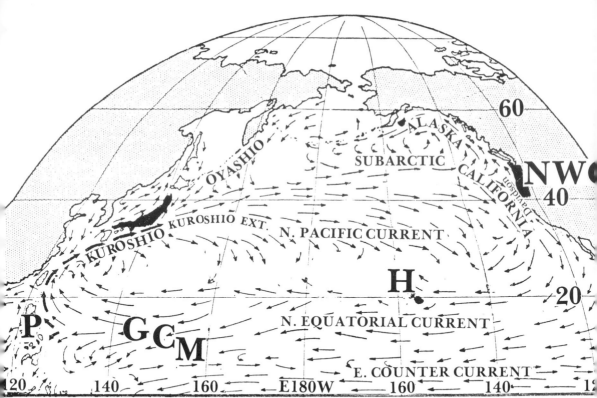

Chart of North Pacific Ocean on Good's Homolosine Equal-Area Projection illustrating major surface currents typical of February-March. Identifying marks: C: Caroline Islands; G: Guam (Mariana Islands); H: Hawaiian Islands; M: Marshall Islands; NWC: Northwest Coast, U.S.A.; P: Philippine Islands.

to do with the rotation of the Earth. There is a gyroscopic, or Coriolis force involved which acts on any water particle in motion. In the Northern Hemisphere, this force as well as the horizontal part of the tidal force, usually rotates in a clockwise sense. As a result of these two influences, tidal currents in the open ocean generally rotate in a clockwise direction north of the Equator, and in a counterclockwise direction south of the Equator. (There are exceptions.)

In many people's minds, an ocean current is a large river of water moving within clearly definable limits. But this is not accurate. A current is made up of many sub-units, the units moving at different speeds, different directions, and at varying depths and widths depending on the season. Scientists (oceanographers) take this conglomeration of more or less descrete sub-units and label them as a current.

Motion of any mass on earth is influenced by the deflecting force of the earth's rotation (Corioli's force) along with other factors, which explains why speed and direction of ocean currents is not constant. Thus, if one could hover above a glass ball and observe its drift, one would see the ball moving at different speeds at different times.

Gyrals in the ocean—huge whirlpools—occur principally where two currents come together causing counterflow at the point of impact. When jetsam and flotsam become caught in such pools, a high velocity wind is needed to break the floating mass out of the pool, over the "edge" so to speak, into a bordering current that will carry the mass away.

It is believed that the discovery of large numbers of glass floats within a very small beach area is a result of this sudden mass movement of debris out of a gyral into a current. The mass continues to float in a clockwise manner and when near the Northwest Coast, if other conditions are right, the whole lot might be cast onto a beach within a relatively short time span.

Referring to the map, note these surface currents, clockwise, from lower right corner. (There are also deep water currents, however it is the surface currents that are of the most interest to beachcombers.)

THE NORTH EQUATORIAL CURRENT of the Pacific Ocean runs from east to west from Central America being made up principally of water from the Equatorial Counter Current and the California Current, which will be further identified shortly. Near the Philippines, the North Equatorial Current divides. One part turns south, and the other, larger portion, bends to the north (clockwise) passing the Philippine Islands and the east coast of Formosa. These warm waters continue in a northeasterly direction where they pass the Ryukyus (Okinawa). At about latitude 30 degrees North the flow again bends to the east, then northeast following the east coast of Japan to about latitude 35 degrees N. *The name KUROSHIO (Japan Current) is particularly applied to the current between Formosa and latitude 35 degrees N.*

Since many Japanese fishing craft operating offshore of their home islands lose their gear into the Kuroshio Current, it has been said that it is the Kuroshio that brings the lost glass balls to the Northwest Coast of the United States. But let us look further.

In agreement with the nomenclature used in dealing with the currents of the Atlantic, oceanographers apply the name "Kuroshio System" *to all branches of the current system generally called the North Pacific Drift* as follows:

1. The KUROSHIO, which we have already detailed as flowing from Formosa to Japan via Okinawa then along the coast of Japan to latitude 35 degrees N.

2. The KUROSHIO EXTENSION. This is a warm flow which is the direct extension of the Kuroshio and flows almost due east to about longitude 160 degrees East. Along this route the Kuroshio Extension splits. The southern fork circles back to join the waters of the Kuroshio between Formosa and Okinawa. Because of the circling back there is a gyral here. The north split becomes:

3. The NORTH PACIFIC CURRENT which continues toward the east and extends to about longitude 150 degrees W. To this point we have basically warm water currents. A flow from the OYASHIO CURRENT, which runs in a southerly direction along the often frigid coast of Kamchatka, intermingles with these warm waters causing strong eddys and a thorough mixing.

On the map, note that the NORTH PACIFIC CURRENT gives way to the

SUBARCTIC ALEUTIAN CURRENT and the CALIFORNIA CURRENT.

The SUBARCTIC CURRENT swirls counterclockwise becoming the ALASKA CURRENT. A tail of the Alaska Current swishes through the Shelikof Strait between Afognak and Kodiak Islands and the Alaska Peninsula.

The flow of the North Pacific Current dips south at about long. 150 W., with a large portion flowing between the Hawaiian Islands and the mainland of North America.

The CALIFORNIA CURRENT is a continuation of the southern split of the Subarctic Current and some portions of the North Pacific Current.

According to Sverdrup, Johnson and Fleming, in *The Oceans,* the name, California Current, is specifically applied to the southward flow between latitude 48 degrees and 23 degrees N., where, as earlier stated, the California Current converges off Central America with the NORTH EQUATORIAL CURRENT. Thus we have completed the basic clockwise circle of currents in the North Pacific Ocean.

Since we are primarily concerned in this observation of ocean currents with the landing of fishing floats along the Northwest Coast, we must also consider the DAVIDSON CURRENT. This current is sometimes called the "culprit" current by beachcombers, since it must be surmounted by other forces before beautiful treasures from the sea can become beached.

The Davidson Current was named for George Davidson, a 19th century

Davidson Current along the Northwest Coast prohibits landing of fishing floats unless sufficient wind is blowing from north-northwest to overcome the current.

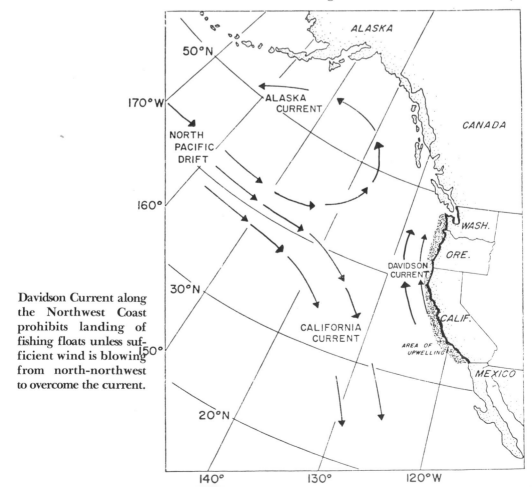

cartographer, who prepared the earliest U.S. Government charts of the west coast. This current flows from *south to north* approximately between lat. 30 degrees to 48 degrees N. The Davidson Current is not a wide current, extending from the coast to perhaps only fifty miles offshore. It is this *nearshore* surface current during the prime float beachcombing season—mid-November to mid-February—that is a factor in curtailing beaching of glass balls. (The wind must also be considered in relation to getting floats across the Davidson Current. We will discuss the wind shortly.)

Here then is the situation. Imagine fishing fleets of several nations with glass, plastic, iron, and aluminum floats supporting nets and long tuna lines covering all of the North Pacific Ocean. Boats are working off Hawaii. There are boats in the Marshalls, East Carolines and Mariana Islands. More boats are off the eastern Philippines and Okinawa. Some home boys are out for just a day's fishing a few miles off the coast of Japan. And others have boats off Kamchatka, some are south of the Aleutians, and men in boats are casting nets between Kodiak and Seattle. On one night imagine one single storm washing over these hundreds of boats thereby dumping thousands of fishing floats of all varieties overboard. See now that all these floats, dumped into the sea at all of the points mentioned, start their drift *clockwise* in the great North Pacific Ocean.

For a home experiment, fill the bathtub to about four inches depth of water. With one hand stir the water in a clockwise motion. When the "current" thus generated seems to be really moving, carefully place a bar of floating soap or a cork on the water. What happens? The floating soap or cork moves with the currents you stirred up. Consider the right end of the tub to be the west coast of the United States. When the floating object begins to swirl around the right end of the tub, place your head near the water level and near the object and blow—hard! If one

Many glass floats are smashed on rocks if there is no beach to receive them.

71

blows hard enough, the "float" will crash against the right end of the tub. *Ah so!* The "glass floats" have just crashed against Northwest Coastal rocks, or landed on a sandy beach — whichever.

It seems then, that the ocean currents play one role of giving just about anything that floats in the sea a chance at beaching along the Northwest Coast. But that chance hinges on three additional factors. 1. The wind, which has just been briefly mentioned. 2. The wind direction. 3. The tide.

Frank B. Kistner, formerly at the University of Wyoming Geology Department, discusses, in an unpublished paper, the importance of the wind as a factor for driving floats ashore. He found that if a glass ball approached the Northwest Coast on the clockwise currents, the float will probably not beach because of the counter-direction of the Davidson. Most everyone can understand that a brisk wind is needed to shove a float across the "culprit" current. Further, it appears that brisk wind is a factor toward assisting a wet, slippery float to stay on the beach once a crashing breaker has thrown it there. Otherwise, as often happens, especially with the rolling-pin shape floats, they roll right back with the receding wave. But how brisk a wind is needed to overcome the alongshore Davidson? Will a good steady wind cause enough drag on a freshly beached ball to allow the wave which brought it to recede without pulling the float back with it?

Still another consideration has to do with what percentage of the ball is extending over the top of the water to catch the wind? Some floats which have leaked water, or those with barnacle-covered nets are often mostly submerged. If the float is severely barnacle-covered, what drag or "keel" effect does this create? The "scientific" beachcombers argue these points whenever they get together.

Kistner concluded that a wind speed of minimum seventeen knots for a minimum of fifteen hours duration, ideally from west-southwest, was necessary to propel a glass float across the Davidson Current. Is there reinforcement for the Kistner wind hypothesis? Oceanographers at the Marine Science Center, Oregon State University, said in a memo to the authors that glass floats could cross the alongshore current "if strong local westerly winds blow for several hours. Wind in any westerly component whether NW or SW should be favorable to beaching floats regardless of whether Davidson Current or California Current is prevailing."

Countless numbers of collectors agree that bellowing northwesterly winds bring in glass fishing floats. But what about south or southwesterlies?

On December 2, 1972, a 10.1-foot tide hit the Oregon coast. The authors, with college-son Dale assisting, reached the beach on the high. We combed the sands for miles while a thirty-five-mile wind howled and whipped. Having been there before, we had in our pretrip homework marked places on a chart known for their high float yield. We also considered reasonably close car parking so no time would be wasted going between beaches. Accordingly, we covered several prime sections of beachs fairly close together. We worked together and we worked apart. We went around old driftwood and we scrounged the sands. Our yield: Dale found an unbroken foreign light bulb and a good length of tangled line from a crab pot. We met only one other beachcomber. He was empty handed. We knew the wind direction—generally southerly. We also knew that the wind speed was pretty high for although we were covered, wherever the sand hit bare skin it stung. But we had no way of measuring the wind velocity while struggling against it on that south Oregon beach. (The cover picture for this book was made during that trip.) We decided to compare notes with a pair of local beachcombers, June and Bill Cook in Bandon.

While they warmed us with hot tea and fruitcake we told of our experience. We watched retired Navy man Bill's anemometer hold between thirty and thirty-five knots with gusts to fifty—all southerly. "No wonder you didn't find anything. The wind is wrong," exclaimed the knowing Bill Cook.

Oregon State University Marine Science Center Drift Bottle Experiments along the Northwest Coast.

This wind, being from the wrong direction, validates the wind direction hypothesis, at least so for our experience on this stretch of beach at that time. We surely had a good tide, the highest of the season to that date. The little light bulb, about an American forty-watt size, had obviously been deposited by a previous storm.

A south wind, without a tilt from the west, would seem then to propel floats in the alongshore current *parallel* with the coast leaving beachcombers almost assured that no floats will land.

We have observed by the Bandon Beach experience of December 20, 1972, that no floats landed in our areas presumeably because the south wind carried them parallel with the beach. But what happens to floating objects in the alongshore current when there is no "sail" effect? Will the alongshore Davidson current move floats *along* the beach and not onto it? To this point consider the Marine Science Center Drift Bottle Experiments.

The Center is engaged in continuing observations of sea conditions. Between

January 1961 and December 1970, oceanographic vessels operating from the Marine Science Center at Newport, Oregon, made eighty-seven cruises. On each trip scientists placed many thousands of special drift bottles into the ocean at specific points. During this ten year period large numbers of these bottles were retrieved from the sea by fishermen and by persons happening on to the bottles along the shore. Each bottle contained an official business reply card asking the

(Above) *R/V Acona,* one of several vessels participating in Drift Bottle launchings at four points of N. Latitude along Oregon coast. (right) Each dot shows position where Drift Bottles were launched. Numbers are distance in miles from coast where launchings took place.

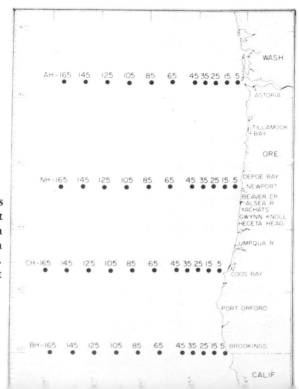

finder to record, "Exact location drift bottle was found, date and hour found" and the name and address of the finder. Each card was numbered. Records were kept for each trip. Recorded were the numbers from the cards, the points and dates of each release. When a bottle-finder returned a card a search for the card's number was made. The finder then received a letter thanking him for returning the card, restating where the finder said he picked up the bottle and the date. The letter then identified which of the several oceanographic vessels had released that particular bottle and exactly where (by latitude and longitude). The letter then told how far in miles the bottle had drifted in how many days and at what speed. As an example:

Bottle No. 208 was picked up off Estevan Point Lighthouse, British Columbia. Bottles had been released from the *R/V Acona* at a point five miles west of Coos Bay, Oregon, on March 21, 1961. Bottle No. 208 traveled 376 miles in less than forty-two days at a rate of 0.374 knots. As the study was for checking *current* direction and speed, bottles were weighted with sand to submerge enough to lessen the influence of the wind.

Returns of cards from within test bottles were received from as far north as Afognak Island, Alaska (1320 miles). The average velocity of the current was about 0.30 knots but a few bottles averaged 1.50 knots.

In a similar experiment conducted by the Honolulu Laboratory of the Bureau of Commercial Fisheries, a sealed beer bottle set adrift near Honolulu in 1961 came ashore near Cannon Beach, Oregon. The bottle had been drifting for more than seven years. The Department of the Interior said in a press release on March 14, 1969, that the beer bottle had drifted a straight-line distance of 3,090 miles. An oceanographer with the Bureau of Fisheries in Honolulu estimated that actual distance traveled was between ten and twelve thousand miles.

This beer bottle may have spent several years swirling around a gyral before a stiff wind drove it into an adjoining current. (*See also* the incident about a drifting coconut that took thirty-one years to beach. (Chapter 13)

In addition to ocean currents, wind direction and speed, are the tides. Observations by and the huge collections of floats that some beach-side residents have picked up following high tides pretty well establish that most floats land on high tides. These residents claim that although occasionally they see glass balls come in on a low tide, such cases are infrequent. The highest tides of the year along the Northwest Coast are during winter months. We therefore offer these conclusions:

For the best chance of finding a glass fishing float one should look on a wide, flat beach, on a high tide in winter when the wind has been bearing from the west for some hours at a speed better than seventeen knots. These are the signals to put on winter garb, grab a big sack and let us go beachcombing! □

Large glass float very deep purple in color shown on display at Netarts-Oceanside-Cape Meares Beachcombers Festival 1976. Although ocean was calm, waves in handblown float cause distortion when scene viewed through the glass. Rocks are off Maxwell Point, northwest of Oceanside. Exposure for such a photograph can be tricky. Make certain exposure meter reads only light projected *through* the float without light from beyond float circumference striking the photo cell of the meter.

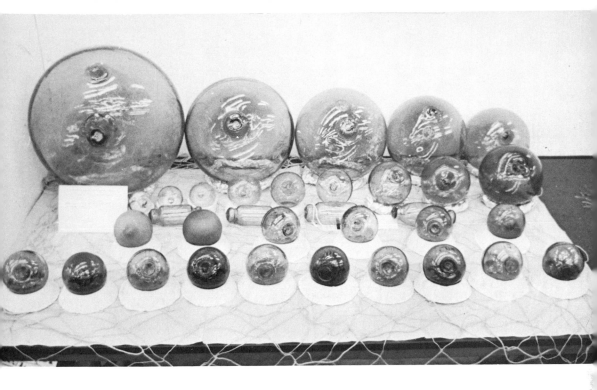

CHAPTER 8

SIZES AND TYPES OF GLASS FLOATS

Depending on what the sea churns up, where one is beachcombing, and in what wind conditions, may determine what size of glass balls will be found.

For some reason, the incidence of small floats predominates along the Northwest Coast. This is not to say that only small floats are to be found—far from it! But the mathematical count of inventories of very large collections demonstrates that far more small size floats are beachcombed than are large ones.

Sizes collected thus far start with a two-inch model—about the size of a golfball. Sizes are irregular up through about five-inches—grapefruit size. The next is a six-, then eight-, ten-, twelve-, thirteen-, fourteen-, fifteen-, sixteen-, eighteen- and even nineteen-inches diameter. Although no standard has been set, floats over about twelve-inches diameter are usually discussed at the beachcombers festivals in circumferences.

Probably the largest float publically displayed to that time, appeared in an exhibit in the 1977 festival at Seaside (Chapter 21). This huge blue-green color glass ball measured exactly sixty-inches circumference!

A beautiful purple float, the color caused by adding manganese dioxide at the factory, displayed in the 1975 festival at Oceanside, was just under sixty-inches.

According to Amos L. Wood, seventy-seven per cent of all floats represented in a large collection on the Long Beach peninsula were not larger than six-inches. In his own collection, Wood sorted eighty per cent in the six-inch-and-under class.

Extra large rolling pin floats are not often found. Smaller rollers of the five to six inch size can be beachcombed but rollers are nowhere as common as the ball shapes.

The tennis ball size (about three inches), accounted for about half of the floats in both collections.

Probably the most common rolling pin shaped floats are in the five to six-inch lengths. These rollers vary in diameter but about one-and-one-half-inches appears the most common. Rollers are findable but not often. When the waves wash them ashore these floats roll to a stop—or near stop—then the receding wave usually carries them back to sea.

Means of attaching nets or ropes around floats at sea has always been a problem, thus many spherical floats have nets installed at the factory on them, some with attaching rings. The rolling-pins, however, usually have knobs molded at each end. These can be said to resemble old style glass insulators used on radio antennas.

In the mathematical cut computed by Wood, only about one or two per cent roller types have been observed. But rollers *do* stay on the sand. At Pacific Beach State Park, Washington, the attendants picked up six rollers in two seasons. Each roller was slightly different in shape and color tint indicating that each was from a different factory and probably lost from different fishing boats.

Classed as a variation from the small rolling pins are the very large, rich-green color, cylinders. At the Seaside festival in 1977, an exhibitor displayed one that was so large he carried it with a shoulder strap. This float was about ten-inches diameter and probably eighteen-inches or more in length. It was very heavy. It was of very thick glass.

Floats of odd shapes have been found but it is believed these are usually errors

Margie Webber and Carol Johnson of Pacific Beach, Washington, look at frosted float beachcombed at Pacific Beach State Park.

in manufacture. Even those of nonstandard shapes are usable, so these too are sold to fishermen. Some of these odd floats resemble half-inflated volley balls. Others are reported to be dew-drop or pear shaped.

While the majority of glass balls are of the light blue-green color there are other colors. The authors have the only 7-Up bottle green small float they have ever seen. One end is pushed in thus giving a flat-on-one-side shape. If totally round, it would have been just under four-inches. This odd-ball was beachcombed about mid-way along the Long Beach peninsula in spring of 1968 by a motel operator. We received it as a gift from him.

Some floats are rough finish on their *inside*, not like the rough outer surface that has been caused by scouring on the sand. How this interior scuffing occurred is not known, but it could have been caused in the making. One such was found at Pacific Beach State Park. Although these floats appear "milky" from a distance, a close look reveals the illusion of white to be in the finish of the glass.

In Japanese glass floats, some milk-white floats exist, as do greens in several varieties. There is a darker blue-green probably more closely resembling turquoise. There are beer-bottle browns. Blue has been seen. Pink is reported. A light gold color, much lighter than the frequent amber, is also reported. There is a brilliant red and a deep burgundy red (wine color) float. The purple was mentioned earlier. Of course some floats are colorless. The different colors are created by adding various elements during manufacture.

In the two CCCP (Russian) glass floats studied by the authors, both are three-and-one-half-inches and have an extremely pale amber cast. Only one of

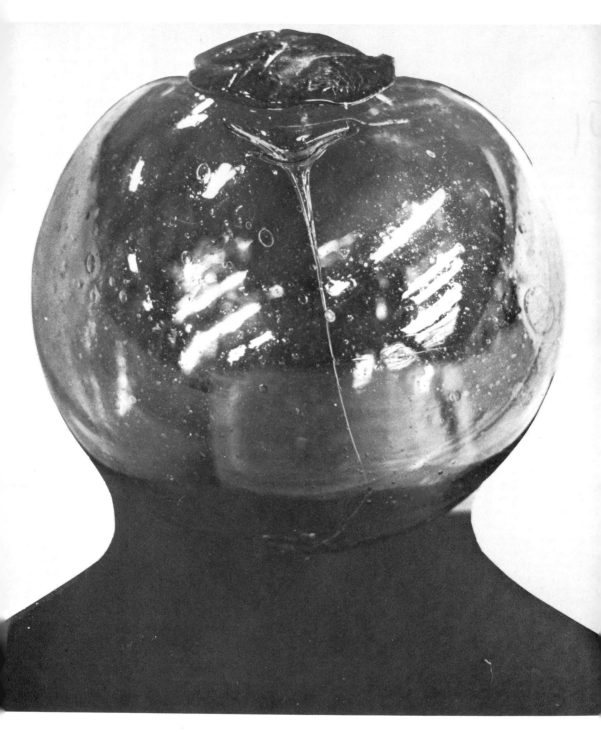

Rare spindle float beachcombed at Seaside, Oregon, by Elinor Johnson.

Margie with 10-inch and 3-inch floats mounted on award-winning display. (right) Driftwood-glass float mobile. Note water in roller.

these floats is earlier reported and that as "clear white." It was picked up at Long Beach, Washington, in 1958. The examples studied by the authors were found on the Kenai Peninsula, Alaska, in 1957. Although Russian in identification, these floats were wartime Lend Lease of 1943 made by Northwestern Glass Company in Seattle. Wood states that "690,000 were manufactured [for] a crab-fishing company of Vladivostok." When and where will King Neptune cough up the rest?

Amos Wood also describes German pale-green glass floats which were imported by Pacific Coast fisherman in the early 1930's. They used these for off-shore and Alaskan fishing. Two sizes were purchased: three- and eight-inch. There is no quantity mentioned but single examples have appeared in 1935 at Cape Alava, Washington, in 1948 on the Oregon coast, and in 1960 in Alaska. The example owned by Lim Fell of Eagle Point, Oregon, made available to the authors for study (along with the to CCCP's just mentioned), was beachcombed on the Kenai Peninsula in 1957.

Probably the most odd of the floats found anywhere can be classed in four categories. 1. Floats with "spindles." 2. Floats with water inside. 3. Two floats stuck together — binaries. 4. Double Balls — one ball inside another.

A spindle in a glass float with a thin, very fragile appearing thread of glass on the inside of the ball extending from the sealing area to a point on the opposite side. The creation of a spindle is believed to be a mishap of manufacturing. Some souvenir floats, especially created with spindles exist, but these have never been in the sea. The probability of finding a spindle, according to seasoned beachcombers, runs about one in 1,500.

The water-logged floats, once believed quite rare, have turned up in many collections. Water inside floats is known in the spheres (balls) as well as in rollers. Water may get inside a float when the sealed navel is imperfect and the float is hauled to depths along with the nets. Pressure may force water into the microscopic openings. When the net with the float is retrieved, the water stays inside as the difference in pressure from the inside is apparently not sufficient to force the water back out. The incidence of floats with water does not seem to be recorded but such floats are indeed treasures. *(See:* Chapter 20)

Binary floats are probably caused when two floats stick together in the cooling process at a factory. Those known appear to be six-inch pairs. Few have been seen along the Northwest Coast and the authors weep a little for not having the $7.50 "in hand cash only" on a day when two teenagers offered one for sale near Bandon in 1971. A binary today is classed as a treasure.

How large does the "bubble" have to be on the inside of the navel of a ball-shaped float to be a true "double ball"? In the tennis ball size floats, the authors' candidate for being called a double ball is a float with a bubble in it about 5/16th-inch diameter. The inner ball looks like a small marble. Some float interiors may have a blister or a hump on the inside of the naval but these cannot be defined as a true inner ball. The incidence of double balled floats is rare, considerably less than that of spindles. ☐

CHAPTER 9

BEWARE OF PHONY FLOATS

Generally, glass floats come across the sea one at a time and are tossed onto the beaches by King Neptune. Therefore, along the Northwest Coast most of the floats offered for sale are genuine and sell in a wide price range. Largely, the price is determined by the law of economics. If the dealer has few floats, up goes the price. Thus, in many instances, when the dealer has been successful with his "beach patrol," in his 4-wheel drive vehicle in the wee hours of the high tide, he might sell for less. Some dealers who are permanent residents of the seashore, stockpile good finds and sell from their pile. Many of these dealers maintain a fairly high price for floats year around regardless of the local happenstance of floats on their beachfront property.

Almost all glass floats offered for sale are Japanese and are of Coke bottle color. (When the authors were in Japan, they saw no evidence of Coke bottles being used for making floats as persons in the U.S. recognize a Coke bottle. The Coke bottles in Japan in 1975 were clear glass, not blue-green! (*See:* Chapter 10.)

Although tourists who seek to buy a glass fishing float may be attracted to brightly colored glass balls hanging from nice, clean, white cord (kite string?), these balls probably have a sticker on them reading, "Made in Hong Kong," "TAIWAN," or "JAPAN." These are the "phonies" that a seasoned beachcomber is aware of. These thin glass, brightly colored globes are usually mass produced as "curios," and come to the U.S.A. in a crate, probably a gross at a time as "merchandise for resale." They are pretty. They are glass balls. They are not fishing floats.

Genuine fishing floats normally have blemishes in the glass. The sphere is not precisely round. The sealing button varies in size and shape with each float. Hand made glass fishing floats are individual—no two just alike. More often than not there is a "trademark," the oriental characters impressed into the sealing button or near it. Impressed trademarks are seldom seen on curio shop phonies. The tourist-trade models of glass balls sometimes have blemishes, but never like those that might have happened when the oriental glass blower hiccupped with the tube in his mouth!

Genuine beachcombed glass floats do not come with fresh, white, kite-string nets. The nets from the sea are thick rope—sometimes nylon. The colors vary but most are "well-used" brown or black. Some floats fresh from the factory, which were lost overboard from a boat soon after purchase, might have lighter color netting, but the netting is thick—never like kite string.

The only red, or pink netting the authors have ever seen is on a float obtained in the Marshall Islands off the islet of Ebeye in the Kwajalein Atoll.

About "phoney phloats" as one sage wrote, "If a curio shop clerk insists that he is selling genuine fishing floats, remember that the real thing surely did not travel thousands of miles in a raging sea then be tossed upon a beach by King Neptune and ground in the sand and still keep its sticker, "Made in Hong Kong". □

The decorated fence at Pacific Beach State Park. All floats shown were beachcombed within a few hundred yards of the fence within a two year period.

CHAPTER 10

WHO BUT THE JAPANESE MAKE FLOATS ?

Quite often one can hear remarks along the beachfront that people are not beachcombing glass floats because "the industry has converted to plastic and all the glass balls have been picked up."

When one compares the numbers of floats lost from fishing vessels and the factors that permit floats to beach (Chapter 7), it must be presumed that if floats are not being found, it is that beachcombers have not been at the right place at the right time.

At this point we should acknowledge that nations other than Japan — including the United States — make and use fishing floats on a regular basis. The Japanese did not invent them. There is evidence that fishermen in Norway used glass for floats sometime during the 1840's. Possibly some floats broke loose and were beachcombed in Denmark and Danish fishermen got ahold of them. Or maybe a Norweigian merchant went to Denmark to sell some. It is not recorded. But it was not until thirty years later that the Danes started making their own.

Japan, who had borrowed many Western ideas during the Meiji period of enlightenment, saw a good thing and has been making glass floats since about 1910. It appears that the United States was forced into making them only because the Pacific War cut off the Japanese supply.

Should a favorite beach yield a sphere that reads, "DURAGLAS" (Owens-Illinois Glass Company, Oakland, California), or "NW" (Northwestern Glass Company, Seattle), this is obviously a "Made in U.S.A." product. But do not be put down that you only found a local product and not a coveted glass ball from Japan. These two American trademarks are rather rare, for only limited production was undertaken.

"Made in Norway" floats have been picked up along the Northwest Coast for

many years. "Republic of Taiwan" have been found. There are floats marked, "Made in England." Glass ball-type floats have been made in China (mainland, pre-World War II), Czechoslovakia, Denmark, France, Germany (both pre- and post-World War II), Scotland, Sweden, and possibly others. Some manufacturers make plastic as well as glass and some make floats of metal. The Norway and "Made in England" floats appear in glass, aluminum, and plastic. The Soviet Union uses glass, marked CCCP, and unmarked eight-inch (rusty) cast-iron balls.

Some floats used by Russian fishermen were "Made in U.S.A." but there is no such mark on the floats. These came from Northwestern Glass Company in Seattle, and were presented to the Soviet government along with other "lend-lease" materials during the Second World War.

Some of the plastic floats, generally a little smaller than a volleyball, come in brown, orange, or black. The names of the country of manufacture is clearly molded into the design. But because a particular float is beachcombed. it would be presumptious to say that the float had been lost from a vessel of the same nationality. On a recent trip to Crescent City, California, the authors saw and photographed many floats lashed to a net which had been set out to dry. These floats were from Norway, Taiwan, England and there was one rusty Russian.

Recently, glass floats of the three-inch size, with protective black, plastic jackets on them, have been beachcombed. The jackets help to eliminate breakage when the floats are winched aboard fishing boats.

At a glance, one might easily conclude that glass floats with Oriental characters are all Japanese floats. But this is not correct. Japanese, Korean, and Chinese writing forms all appear the same — Oriental — to the unknowing. Japanese has several forms, the simplest being katakana(kah-teh-kah-neh) which is used on typewriters, can be tapped on a telegraph key, and is now appearing on fishing floats.

Chinese characters, called kanji (kahn-gee) were borrowed by the Japanese hundreds of years ago at a time when the Japanese did not have their own written form. Kanji, as used in Japan today, has been modified so much the Chinese can no longer read it, and the Japanese cannot read the original Chinese. Both forms of kanji appear on glass fishing floats. It is assumed that Chinese kanji on glass floats is an indicator that the floats was manufactured in (mainland) China before the formation of the Republic of China (Taiwan) in 1949 on the island of Formosa. The present manufacture of floats in Taiwan is believed to be principally plastic. These are easy to identify for each float the authors have inspected was marked in

(A) Bill Ireland picked up this "Made in Norway" aluminium float at Gleneden Beach State Park. (B) Pre-World War II German float found in Alaska. (C) Taiwan (Republic of China) plastic float from Crescent City, California. (D) Russian Float from Vladivostok, manufactured in Seattle, found in Alaska. (E) Russian glass float probably made in Soviet Union. Hammer and sickle is undoubtedly most rare of all marks, beachcombed near Waldport, Oregon, in 1945. (F) Rare marking in Chinese kanji *and* Japanese katakana from Sasa Co. in Japan. Beachcombed by (G) Verna Van Zante at Peacock Spit, Cape Disappointment, on February 15, 1977.

(Left to right):
NW Glass Co.
CCCP (Soviet)
Prewar German
Duraglas

Chinese (kanji) as well as in English, "Made in Taiwan."

Glass floats of Korean manufacture might have Sino-Korean characters which the Chinese would pronouce one way and the Koreans another. The Korean alphabetic Han'gul (hahn-gull) script is said to be in use on glass floats (however the authors have not observed any thus far.) Han'gul, to the untrained eye, could be said to *loosely* resemble katakana in form but to a Japanese or Korean, katakana and Han'gul are *not* alike and usually neither person can read the other's language.

It has often been rumored that brown floats are made from salvaged (recycled) beer bottles and that other color glass is used for other color floats. When the authors were in Japan in the summer of 1975, we spent several hours at the factory of the Okuhara Glass Company. We observed that the use of old bottles was not a rumor.

In one box, the size of which would take a fork-lift truck to hoist, we found thousands of pieces of broken, green 7-Up bottles ready to be melted and poured. In another box were neatly broken pieces of clear glass bearing trade names "Bireley's Orange" and "Pepsi."

On that August afternoon, the thermometer on the shaded wall of the glass company read about thirty-five degrees C. (100 degrees F.) Inside the factory, with the furnaces blazing, the temperature was much hotter. We watched young men (stripped to the waist) blowing glass balls at the end of long tubes. Being inside a glass factory in Oriental August humidity is just about as opposite to the fresh crisp breeze of the Oregon coast as one can get. Nevertheless, the authors, fascinated, stayed in the factory as the chance for a repeat visit would not come soon.

Using the sign language, and with the help of our hired, friendly taxidriver-guide who knew a little English, we learned that the firm makes all kinds of glass objects including jars, artifacts, and fishing floats. We noted that the factory makes glass balls for two purposes. 1. For fishermen. After the blowpipe is removed, the hole is sealed *inward* to yield a smooth surface all over the outside of the glass ball. 2. For artifacts. These floats have the seal *outward*. The final curing (temperature reducing process), for display floats (globes) in the fire-brick furnace, is done intermittently with blasts of cold air to form a wrinkled finish.

As a souvenir of our visit we purchased a bright, 7-Up-bottle-green, rough textured float, the size of a volley ball. This is the gem of our collection. ☐

CHAPTER 11

HOW MANY FLOATS STILL IN THE SEA ?

If Japanese fishermen discountinued using glass floats and adopted some other method of net and long-tuna-line support, how many floats would there be left in the sea? Amos Wood completed a comprehensive survey on this question. This included personal interviews with long-time residents of selected beaches. He considered the total number of floats manufactured over a fifty-four year period, a close estimate of the number lost by fishermen in the North Pacific Ocean, weather and tide records, the estimated number of floats broken on rocks, and the total of survivals on the beaches available to whomever happened along.

He inspected float collections owned by those who had tramped the same sections of beach for years for these collections were larger than the ordinary. He reasoned that the more floats found in the same area over a long period should provide a valid base for depth study. A collector on the Long Beach peninsula, Ralph McGough, picked up about three thousand floats in four years. In one seven month period, McGough beachcombed about four hundred. Wood determined, after investigation, that the man's findings were only about thirty per cent of the total actually found in McGough's regularly patrolled four mile stretch. Others who happened along got the rest.

Mr. Wood reported that his survey revealed ninety-seven per cent of the floats in the North Pacific Ocean are Japanese. He wrote, "Roughly, forty per cent of all Oriental glass fishing floats ever lost are probably still out there in the Pacific.... Using all the data...and what I consider realistic...I conclude that the North Pacific Ocean still retains approximately *ten million* Japanese fishing floats."

He concludes:

For each one hundred glass floats lost in the North Pacific Ocean each year:
31 are broken on the rocks.
27 are beached intact, buried in the sand, are beachcombed, or remain.
42 are still out in the ocean.

At the rate the North Pacific Ocean retains lost floats, and since factories of many of the nations which have fishing fleets operating in the North Pacific manufacture floats, it hardly stands that "all of the glass balls have been picked up." □

Many beachcombed glass objects, particularly floats with original netting, are quite dirty—some with oil impregnated rope. Margie cleans her large float from Tinian by first soaking float overnight in water with mild dishwashing detergent. Keeping float submerged for period of time can be a problem. One method is to place a wooden box that fits within the sink over float weighting the box with bricks thus forcing float to stay under water. Rinse with warm water. Float washing is best done in summer when netted floats can be set in sun for several days so net will thoroughly dry.

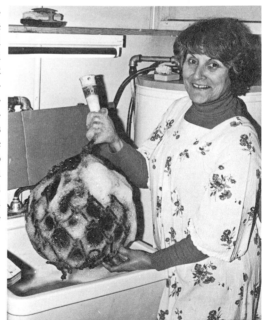

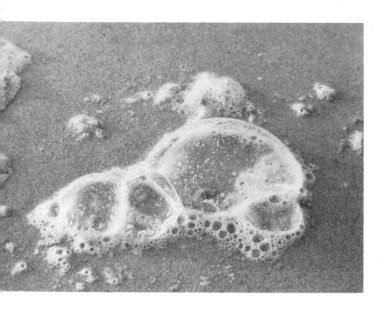

CHAPTER 12

EXPERIENCES WHILE BEACHCOMBING

One beach wanderer from Neskowin, Oregon, wrote, "Yes, I picked up seven floats in two days after a series of storms. Most were quite a way up in dry sand territory probably because of the extreme high tides. They were all glass. One was about forty-five-inches diameter. And I was lucky because I also found a six-inch rolling pin float."

A man from Lincoln City was forced to abandon his find. He waded out to a mass of seaweed, steel cable, a large piece of cut lumber, and several eight-inch metal floats. But he was unable to retrieve these Russian cast-iron balls because the mass was all tangled and much too heavy for him to manage. By the time he returned with help, the outgoing tide had taken the whole batch back out to sea.

A fellow stumbled over what he thought at first was a rock sticking out of the sand. It had an odd look about it so he dug it up. He later learned he had salvaged a fifty-million-year-old molar from a mastodon!

Some people can hit the beaches at every opportunity yet *never* find a glass float. If this has happened to you, hold on — your day could be tomorrow!

A woman had lived in a house overlooking the beach for several years. She had never seen a Japanese glass float other than at a friend's home or in curio shops. Late one night, not feeling quite well, she went for a walk on the beach just to get a little fresh air. Down the beach from her place, she spotted a small dark object during those moments when the moon was not behind a sky full of broken clouds. She did not pay much attention until a few seconds later when she saw another blob bobbing in the lazy surf. And then she saw another. The moon slipped from behind a cloud. The sudden eeriness from above was reflected back at her dozens of times within an instant. She was nearly surrounded with glass balls!

Although she was dressed only in a light robe, she picked up as many as she could holding them in her clothing as gathering laundry into an apron. She trudged back to her home. Then she went back to the beach and again packed her gown with all it would hold. She made trip after trip until near dawn when she finally sat down to count and sort her sea-born treasures. Seventy-five elusive Japanese hand-blown spheres she had gathered, all because she could not sleep and had gone for a walk on the beach. But, she related to the authors, "I have not seen a single float since!"

One of your authors will probably never live down his decision not to wade into the surf at Whisky Run Beach along the Oregon coast one February day. Just out of reach was a fully roped, basketball-size Japanese float. What a beauty! But that float just would not come in! To wade out, alone, with no help immediately nearby, we believe would have been foolhardy.

While beachcombing in March 1977, a couple recovered a lost metal key-tag from old Tent City, Bayocean, Oregon. During the early part of this century, there was a resort community on Bayocean (Tillamook) Spit. After years of serious erosion of the sand which caused many buildings to tumble into the sea, a severe winter storm broke through the spit in November 1952. Tent City had earlier been converted to cottages. In the erosion and washout, all of the cottages, a three story hotel and other buildings went down. The area can be reached for beachcombing from the highway west of Tillamook. The recovery of the Tent City key-tag is an important historical treasure.

Beachcombers usually have their minds on a specialty be it glass floats, driftwood, agates, or whatever, and are sometimes not knowledgeable about some other items which King Neptune might toss upon the sands. Within the realm of probability are items to be hopefully, *not stumbled upon*. These are relics of past wars. Like glass floats, torpedoes and mines — some still deadly — come to rest along

(Page 92 left) Margie beachcombed this section of a small boat from the beach at Gold Beach. A check with the Oregon Marine licensing office brought name and address of former owner who said boat was lost from mooring along Rogue River during flood. (right) Youth often sell floats to tourists along Oregon Coast Highway. (above) Foggy beach at Cape Blanco State Park. Beach collects much driftwood but is too steep to keep many glass floats from rolling back into the ocean with receeding waves.

the tidelines.

Few torpedoes have come ashore in recent years but when they do, as with mines, the explosives experts appear somewhat reticent to say much about them. Little newspaper mention of these potentially deadly "beachcombed" pieces of military hardware may be the reason so few people realize a hazard exists. Residents along the coast have declared within the authors' hearing, "The war was thirty years ago. The likelihood of finding anything from the war on the beach is remote." One such orator was a school teacher who seldom went beachcombing.

Just a few months before that judgement was rendered, a couple was beachcombing near the south jetty of the Columbia River. It was May 1976. The fellow, who is interested in rocks, poked at a "rock." "I picked it up, gingerly, and I looked at it. The object was several inches long and it seemed heavier in one end. With a little chipping the 'rock' broke. In one end was a piece of steel with a metal band around it. I took it to the Army Ordnance people at Vancouver Barracks the next week. It was identified as a 37mm shell."

The former gunnery range for Fort Stevens was just behind the hill where the shell was recovered thirty-one years after the war.

Also in 1976, during work on the renovation of the harbor defense battery by the Oregon State Parks and Recreation Department, a casing from a 75mm shell was recovered near the beach. It occurs that during the war there had been a 75mm (3-inch) gun position at the base of the south jetty.

Incidentally, during World War II when the Coast Guard maintained armed patrols along the Northwest Coast's beaches, some of the Guardsmen rounded up hundreds of glass floats then used them for target practice!

Wartime ordnance continues to be a potential problem along the Northwest Coast. Specifically, floating mines appear to be the hazard most likely to be encountered. Loosely speaking, many mines look a little like streamlined ashcans,

James Seeley White beachcombed this Soviet packing case on Beverly Beach then converted it into a hassock. Inscription says in part, "Glass. Handle with Care." "Petropavlosk."

94

Floating ordnance often deadly, travels the same currents as do glass fishing floats. Mine shown was identified as of Soviet origin, came to rest on Tillamook County beach near Cape Meares where it exploded.

or huge fishing floats. Some have points (detonator contacts) sticking out from the body. Some have handles and there may be a section of anchor chain attached.

On the Oregon coast, a mine officially identified as of Soviet origin, came to rest on a Tillamook County beach. It had followed the same currents as the glass floats. The mine was spotted by local residents who quickly told the Coast Guard about it. The Coast Guard responded, staked it out then left to summon a Navy demolitions team. But the tide did not wait for them. As the water deepened, it refloated the mine. The mine rolled down the beach. It hit a rock. *BAM !*

No one was hurt. A resident a quarter-mile away still has a cracked main beam in his home. Window glass salesmen had a field day.

In the fall of 1974 while fishing off the port of Brookings, Oregon, the fishing vessel *Pam Bay* radioed the Coast Guard that there was an object in their net thought to be a mine. It was. The Coast Guard and Navy, working together, carefully dropped what was identified to be a Japanese mine from World War II into a small skiff. An explosive charge was attached then the skiff was set adrift with its deadly load. When the *Pam Bay* and the Coast Guard boat were a good distance away, a radio charge blew the old mine and the skiff sky high. How long would it have taken the mine to wash ashore along the Oregon coast? That would be anyone's guess.

On the Long Beach peninsula several homeowners have placed brightly painted spheres on the tops of fence posts around their yards. What are these spheres, tourists inquire? These balls were once rusty Russian iron floats that were beachcombed a few yards away. The incidence of Russian floats appears to be greater along the Washington shore than along Oregon, and the Russians are losing other than just rusty balls. Celia LaFleur, beachcombing at Ocean Shores, picked up a borsch box. Jim White of Portland carried home a Russian shipping

Dogs who go beachcombing should have salty sand washed from feet at end of the romp.

case which he promptly converted into a hassock.

The six miles of beach at Ocean Shores, Washington, have always been highly regarded by seekers of glass floats and other jetsam and flotsam. Margaret L. Rasmussen, who lives there, compiled statistics about the growth of the town and some beach activities for the period 1959 through 1974. Then the Friends of the Ocean Shores Library put all of the data into a book. Here are some "Bonanza[s] on the beach!"

● Literally millions of pieces of wood, from matchbox size up to saw timber, plus doors, tables, bric-a-brac, and of course glass balls suddenly landed on the beach. (1965)

● Three local men went looking for floats Jan.1. Larry, and Nick Tommer and Harley Bottoroff picked up fifty-two. They had to quit only because they could stuff no more into their International Scout. One week later Bob, Simon and Don Potts and Mike Fisher met the 1 a.m. incoming tide. With flightlight beams seeking reflections, the fellows *snared fifty-seven balls in five hours.* (1965)

● A drift bottle released on Jan. 24, 1966 off the coast of Oregon by Oregon State University was found at Ocean Shores Feb. 12. It had traveled 140 miles in nineteen days. (1966)

● Wreckage of the *West Wind,* 32-foot trawler, hit the beach in early morning Aug. 27. Coast Guard rescued the skipper Arne Hill. (1966)

● Big lumber washup—dimension lumber—hundreds of thousands of pieces. Salvagers built new homes, etc. Profits for haulers with logging trucks, dump trucks on beach loading up. Source unknown—no recent ship disasters. (1970)

● Grays Harbor buoy No. 6 beached due to forty-five to fifty mile windstorm.

● Large log raft claimed by chainsaw-carrying-beachcombers in front of main beach approach road. (1971)

● Coast Guard marker buoy, bottom weight 7,600 pounds, blown onto beach. (1972)

Ocean Shores, Washington

- Storms and tides ripped out about one hundred feet road, demolished sixty feet of North Jetty. (1973)
- Four emergency telephones were installed within walking distance of beach—connects with police station. (1973)
- Live whale beached. Sent to Seattle then to Sea World, San Diego. (1973)
- *Velella* by the millions in July [but no mention of floats]. (1973)
- "Hands Off Stray Logs" warning posted. Defines difference between driftwood and "merchantable - branded logs." (1973)
- Heavy rush of driftwood onto beach, winds up to seventy-five miles per hour. (1973)

There are countless other reportable experiences relating to beachcombing that occur every year along the Northwest Coast. In this chapter, we have presented experiences that are a lot of fun as well as some examples of activities that to those unaware are potentially dangerous. People out for the fun of beachcombing need to be alert to the realities of seashore situations, and like the Coast Guard, *Semper Paratus,* be "always ready" to handle whatever one comes upon. □

CHAPTER 13

The Miracle of the Coconut

ヤシの実を流した
故山之内辰四郎さん

Late Mr. Tatsushiro Yamanouchi
who dropped the coconut into sea.

For decades, the suspense connected with the possibility of finding an urgent note in a bottle from a castaway has quickened the pace of beachcombers. With thousands of fishing boats, pleasure craft, and freighters now on the oceans, there are lots of bottles thrown overboard. But do any have messages in them? While the incidence of notes is very small, they surely do exist and, on occasion, the content is amazing.

We remember the drift bottle experiments (Chapter 7) by the Marine Science Center. Each bottle contained a tag with request that the finder fill in the time and place where it was found and return the card to the University.

Vacationers on cruise ships frequently toss bottles overboard with notes in them. On a recent trip in Mexican waters and through the Panama Canal, Amos and Elaine Wood put dozens of bottles into the water from the stern of the ship. Each bottle had a note asking that the finder please send retrieval data to them. At this writing, no retrievals have been announced.

There is another incident where a bottle with a note was beachcombed, yet the bottle had never been put into the sea. In 1932 a teacher helped sixteen children plant a tree to commemorate the 200th birthday of George Washington. This was in the school yard at Bayocean, Oregon. Twenty-seven years later the tree was uprooted by coastal erosion. What had once been a school yard almost three-quarters-of-a-mile from the ocean, was now the beach.

Mrs. Delores Snyder, who lived at Cape Meares in 1959, was beachcombing when she spotted a broken bottle. She bent over to investiage it and found a smudged note in the remains of the bottle that told of the planting. The validation for the planting comes from Bob Watkins, in 1932 a member of the class and currently a resident at Cape Meares, Oregon. Bob told the authors, "As I remember it, we were supposed to plant an apple tree. But 1932 was a pretty rough year and we couldn't afford an apple tree so we planted an alder."

Sadakichi Oka beachcombed 31-year-old coconut then spent months in locating Mrs. Kiyoko Yamanouchi, widow of writer of letter discovered inside coconut.

If a glass fishing boat, a bottle, or anything else that floats does not beach when it approaches the Northwest Coast it might take the long ride—15,000 miles all around the circuit before it can get another chance at the same beach.

It is nearly impossible to estimate how long any object will take to make the circle because speeds of the currents vary. An object along the Oregon coast might move at three miles per day, while the same float off Tokyo might move ten miles in a day. Tests indicate an object will go about five miles a day in mid-ocean. Should the floating object get caught in a gyral it could make the trip much longer. The North Pacific Ocean's Eastern Gyral is massive. This phenomena is noted near the Hawaiian Islands. But there are gyrals of a lesser size that can also contain floating objects.

A report reached the authors in August 1976 about an amazing beach-combing incident in which a gyral may have played a part. We investigated and discovered that:

Tatsushiro Yamanouchi, 36 (in 1944), a civilian war worker, had been sent to the Philippines. He had evidently been there for some time. One day in Manila he met an Army corporal who was a medic attached to an Imperial Japanese Navy hospital ship. The men discovered that their homes in Japan were only about five miles apart and near Izumo City on the Japanese Sea. Because the mail between the Philippines and Japan was deteriorating, the medic, Masaichi Iizuka, agreed to hand carry letters between Yamanouchi and his wife. Mrs. (Kiyodo) Yamanouchi also sent homemade rice cakes to her husband via the Corporal.

In June 1944, Iizuka told his friend that his ship would be leaving the Philippines for the last time so he would not be back. A few weeks later Yamanouchi wrote to Iizuka expressing his intense desire to return to Japan for he missed his homelife and his family. He also said that he and others planned to hide in the jungle when the Americans (invasion) came. Yamanouchi placed the letter inside a coconut, scratched Iizuka's address on one side, then put his own name on the other side. He threw the coconut into the Philippine Sea from Luzon on July 10, 1944. (American forces landed at Leyte in October.) The current into which Yamanouchi's coconut letter carrier splashed was the North Equatorial. His "mail" was started on its long journey toward Japan.

Thirty-one years later, Sadakichi Oka, 44, a contractor, was fishing from the beach at Taisha machi, on the Japanese Sea. It was the 25th of July 1975. He saw a coconut floating in the water, waded over to it and retrieved it. There was crude carving on the coconut but it could not be read. Oka took it home. Three days later the coconut had dried enough for Oka to read Iisuka's name and address in nearly Izumo City. The carving on the other side was not readable. Oka went to Izumo but he could not locate Iizuka. He eventually found him in another town and delivered the coconut. Iizuka did not remember anyone in his old town, but he had a list of old friends. By now he had opened the coconut and discovered the letter. He also found Yamanouchi's name on his list. Iizuka felt an urgency about completing the delivery even though it was thirty-one years later, so he went to Izumo but learned that the Yamanouchi house had been torn down. He returned home but made inquiries about Yamanouchi's wife and family.

On March 2, 1976, eight months and five days after the coconut had been beachcombed, Kiyoko Yamanouchi, then 65, traveled to see Izuka whom she had been told was looking for her. She took some of her husband's letters with her. She had always told friends, "My husband will be coming home soon for he has a great desire to do so."

On meeting Iizuka, she compared her old letters with the new one. Then wept. Finally she whispered, "It is his writing."

Investigation by the government found that the comments in Yamanouchi's 1944 letter matched the situation at the time. They also learned that Tatsushiro Yamanouchi died in the jungle about one year later—the summer of 1945.

Widow Yamanouchi returned to her present home in Izumo just a few blocks from where Iizuka had looked for her. She gathered her four grown children and told them that their father's need to come home was so intense that, "The coconut floated over the waves and finally landed on our home beach because the great desire had reached the heavens." During the all night Buddhist memorial service Kiyoko Yamanouchi proclaimed, "My husband's spirit has come home at last."

The coconut had been at sea for thirty-one years, traveled a straight-line distance of 3000km (about 1,900 miles), then landed on a beach close to Yamanouchi's home town. Had it been caught in a gyral? When beachcombed, the coconut had no barnacles on it!

On March 11, 1976, *Yomiuri Shimbun,* on which this account is based, published the story. Their headline: "MIRACLE OF COCONUT ROUTE."

Beachcombers who read these anecdotes will surely quicken their pace when they see a bottle (or a coconut) cast upon the beach by King Neptune. □

Pelican Beach State Park south of Crescent City.

CHAPTER 14

DRIFTWOOD OF ALL KINDS AND SIZES

One can find driftwood in just about every cove and estuary and it comes in every shape and condition imaginable. Trunks of trees, root pods and limbs are sculptured by the grinding they get on the sandy beaches while being pushed around by a very forceful King Neptune. And driftwood becomes sunbleached from years of being left alone high and dry on a beach. Driftwood has become so plentiful in some areas that it has been declared a hazard. In the 1960's the governor of Oregon wanted the State Highway Division to clear the beaches of all dangerous logs. But a Highway Department engineer said there was no practical way to get rid of driftwood for the sea would just throw up more on the next storm. He told the governor that to try to control the driftwood would be like trying to control the weather.

In recent years, the subject has come up again concerning what to do with the driftwood. In Oregon, some sections of the beach have been experimentally "logged" under permits issued by the State. But geologists get frayed nerves with such beach activity, many claiming that to remove the logs, especially in large quantities from some beaches, may tip the balance of the fragile and sand dune leaving it open for washout during the next big storm.

Probably the most unthoughtof potential danger to beachcombers concerns driftwood. These dangers can be summarized in two statements. 1. Logs which land on the beach by wave action are unstable. To climb on logs, especially those that are still wet from the last storm, might cause one to slip. Further, since the logs

101

are merely "resting" on the beach they may not be in balance and will or roll when someone jumps on one. Many of these logs weigh tons. If a log tips and a beachcomber falls and the log rolls over him—that may be the end of one beachcomber. 2. Often youths hop onto a log in the surf and try to ride them onto the sand. These heavyweight logs may float easily in the water but with the sudden weight of a person climbing aboard logs have been seen to tip then buck like a wild horse. If the rider is knocked off and gets rolled by the log—that too can become the end of a beachcomber.

Log On Beach Kills Portlander

LINCOLN CITY (UPI) — Sue Molstrom, daughter of Mrs. Dale Molstrom, 3445 NE Clackamas St., Portland, was killed Sunday night when she was struck by a log as she fled from a wave on the ocean beach here.

Police said the girl was on the beach near the Inn at Spanish Head with a brother and friends when the accident occurred about 10 p.m.

Beach walker hit by wave tossed logs

LINCOLN CITY (UPI) — Therese Dixon, 50, Eugene, suffered multiple fractures of the legs and arms Monday afternoon when struck by logs hurled by waves at Lincoln Beach south of here.

She was taken to the C Samaritan Hospital Portland where she was lis in fair condition.

She had been walking alo the beach when the mishap (curred about 4:30 p.m.

Log Kills Woman

SEASIDE (UPI) — Ruth Frost, 65, Seaside, was killed Saturday when a large wave hurled a log 150 feet from the surfline here. She was walking the beach with friends, and gale warnings were up. Others in her party were not injured.

Every season there are numerous newspaper articles about injuries and deaths on the beaches caused by logs. When walking in the accumulated driftwood, probably the first thing one might do is choose a piece for a walking stick. Before stepping on a log, give the log a shove with the walking stick to test for stability.

Seasoned beachcombers choose a length of driftwood to use as a walking stick and prod. Scene near end of South Jetty, Coquille River (Bandon). Metal is part of hull from grounded ship—the ship later filled with rock to extend the jetty. "Prodder" is Richard Webber, eldest son of authors.

Beachcombers with rubber soled shoes will generally have no difficulty keeping a footing on *dry* logs and *dry* rocks. However wet rubber shoes, and leather soles wet or dry even on dry logs or rocks, are slippery.

The woods specialist will probably have his favorite beach on which to search for the very piece he is wanting. Some beaches tend to collect logs—Salishan Spit—other beaches "specialize" in twigs—Patrick's Point. Most have a variety of all kinds and sizes. In certain areas of the Northwest Coast, beaches collect the woods of that area. The rivers of Northern California discharge redwood. In Southern Oregon, Myrtlewood (California Laurel) is frequently seen. Douglas Fir, madrone, oak, pines, cedar and other types are prolific along the beaches of the Northwest Coast. (*See*: Appendix D.)

Logs lost in rivers float to the sea to be distributed along beaches as driftwood on high tides.

An interesting twist to the nomenclature of driftwood came to light in recent months. The question is asked: What is the difference between driftwood as commonly understood, and "tumblewood"?

A Southern California wood artist, Harold Wakeman, makes these points:

> Tumblewood is natural wood fragments that tumble down turbulent rivers eventually to be deposited along the ocean's beaches. Tumblewood takes on a unique worn character as it sloshes against rocks in a river then is burnished on sandy beaches by the tides. Tumblewood is untouched wood, that is, it has never been handled by man. Tumblewood is without nail holes, saw marks, or other man-made infringements on its beauty.
>
> Driftwood, on the other hand may be flotsam—a piece from a boat; or jetsam—something made of wood in this case, that was thrown or washed overboard from a boat or ship such as wooden vegetable crates, ship's carpenter scrap, dimension lumber, furniture, etc. Also, pieces from sunken ships. Or sections of, or beams from, wharfs that have broken loose during a storm and eventually land on a beach. Wood that bears marks showing that the piece went through a sawmill or was used in any constuction does not have the flavor of "tumblewood."

In the making of artifacts from beachcombed wood, it stands that the artist

(Left to right) "Tumblewood" artist Harold Wakeman created "The Baron." Authors assembled "Parakeet" then photographed around 5 a.m. with low-angle sunlight. Barbara Watkins, driftwood artist of Cape Meares, demonstrates technique at Beachcomber's festival. (below) Bert with section of boat found on Salishan beach.

could say of his work, "This was created from tumblewood. It is completely natural. Nothing has been added to it. No mechanical devices or abrasive materials or surface coating applied by man have ever touched it." One would need to be vigilant in choosing his beachcombed example then in building a display piece to meet all the requirements of the "tumblewood artist." Once beachcombers have been informed, they can quickly see the difference between tumblewood and ordinary driftwood.

But "driftwood" is the general term for just any piece of wood that is tossed upon the beach by the sea. Beautiful artifacts can be created be the wood left completely natural, or gouged, sawn, chisled, sanded, varnished, waxed, burned, or painted.

Some driftwood artists make miniature pieces no bigger than a minute. Others make table pieces and wall mountings. Still others, who do their artistry with a chain saw, cut life-size figures from long, heavy logs. The imagination can run wild when thinking of things to do with, and ways to display driftwood.

With driftwood, if an artist makes a mistake it is still not a total loss if the home has a wood stove or a fireplace! □

Mermaid carved from driftwood, Crescent City. (right) Margie picked driftwood for campfire and...

. . .Bert hauls the sacked firewood to nearby Bullard's Beach State Park campsite. (below) Beaches are patrolled regularly not only for motor vehicle violations but as fire guards. Here Oregon State Police put out unattended fire left from picnic. Fires in driftwood are prohibited on some beaches.

CHAPTER 15

ARE YOU SAFE WHILE BEACHCOMBING ?

A raging sea, some say, is King Neptune on a spree.

For beachcombers, the greatest potential hazard is the sea itself. When one stoops to sort a pile of driftwood, or to look for agates, do so *facing* the water.

Waves are totally unpredictable and there is no substitute for being constantly alert for them. There is no validity to the old story that "the seventh wave is the biggie" for the larger and more dangerous waves cannot be predicted. Even a little wave, a two or three footer, can knock down a person. A toddler, out of an adult's reach for even a minute, would have little chance in the surf. There are "sneaker" waves even on outgoing tides. *Never turn your back on the sea!*

Most beachcombers, especially those seeking only driftwood, do not carry tide tables. In a random check of persons sorting through the driftwood at Bandon State Park, only one had a tide chart in pocket. Three had consulted a tide chart before they came. They lived nearby. Over thirty questioned acknowledged they did not know how to read a tide chart although one of them had a chart along.

Incoming tides can come in quickly on very flat beaches. A big log floats mostly submerged and from a flat beach floating logs are hard to see. Even on ebb tide it pays to keep one eye on the surf for these outgoing tides still tumble logs.

As detailed earlier, it is unwise to stand on or even get near a log that is in the surf, or on wet sand near the tide line. An unpredictable wave might pick it up, toss it or roll it, thus anyone who happens to be in the way is risking injury or death.

Undoubtedly the safest way to beachcomb is by pairs or in a group. Avoid being on the beach alone. If one must walk the beach alone, tell those in camp, or your motel manager where you expect to go and how long you expect to be gone.

Scout leaders found quite early in their program that a "buddy system" was a good means of mutual assistance. If one of the Scouts became injured or ill, the other could go for help. Likewise in old time armies, each squad had a get-away-man in case the squad was pinned down by enemy fire. A lone beachcomber has no help available except for the chance passerby. As best, there is no guarantee that a passerby will "be involved."

Be realistic about how big a load of water-soaked driftwood one should try to carry back to the car. Wet wood is heavy. Overexertion, especially if one leads a usually sedentary life, might bring on heart attack. Some suggest if there is *any* trouble, call the Coast Guard!

The SEMPER PARATUS (*Always Ready*) United States Coast Guard has as its first mission, Search and Rescue (SAR). There are over 12,000 miles of coast-line, tens of thousands of small boats in addition to ocean liners, therefore there are many Coast Guard installations along all of the coasts of the United States. On the Northwest Coast the Coast Guard is ready with man-power and with equipment to assist persons or boats and ships in distress. But how does one call the Coast Guard when alone in a cove and about to be caught by an incoming tide ? The Coast Guard, to effect a rescue, must be notified, must get to where the trouble is located then be able to offer specific assistance while the victim is still able to respond. This takes time.

To consider that "the sea is beautiful and restless but I am quick on my feet" is not enough. Rather, as John Millington Synge (1871-1909) wrote, "A man who is not afraid of the sea will soon be drowned."

Beachcombers can often avoid becoming newspaper headlines and death statistics, by being alert to situations before conditions get out of hand.

WHERE ARE MY DRY SOCKS ?

The Northwest Coast is noted for its ever changing weather, therefore, one of the easiest ways to spoil a session of beachcombing is to be improperly outfitted. The wise tramper of the sands is carefully equipped. Since one depends on his feet to get him about the beach, proper footwear is essential. Socks, without holes, are part of good foot packaging. A usual fun-type question asked by many Scout leaders before camping trips: "How many pairs of socks do you need at camp?" The unanimous answer is shouted: "Always one more pair than we brought!" One authority claims if he can keep his head warm and his feet dry he has it made for the day, for to be wet during a winter storm is not only miserable, it is also potentially unhealthful.

Equally essential on a long beach hike is something to drink and an energy boosting snack. A drink the writers keep in an all metal vacuum bottle is hot, unsweetened tea. During those winter beachcombing forays, hot tea is a welcome drink. It also serves in emergencies. Use tea to rinse sand from between fingers and toes, or to wash a windshield. Unsugared hot tea makes an excellent face wash after being blasted during a severe wind and rain storm. Should one get fingers singed while toasting marshmallows, tea can be used as first aid as it contains tannin. Try tea as a rinse for a sunburned back, especially if there is sand clinging to it. (For making tea at the beach *see:* Appendix A.)

Many hikers find that the best all-around thirst quencher is a fresh orange. Other forms of quick energy are Pillsbury Food Sticks and Nature Valley Granola Bars. These products come individually packed and are easy to keep in a pocket.

Probably the most illadvised snack for hikers anywhere is chocolate, for chocolate brings on thirst in many people. (Avoid granola bars with chocolate coating.) To keep thirst down, try a stick of chewing gum.

Many beachcombers claim they have better success and become less tired when they do their walking with shoes on. Those who insist upon going barefooted may injure a foot and all too frequently spend their vacation laid up. About the most dangerous item for a bare footer to step on, other than glass, seems to be a lid from a flip-top drink can. Such beverage cans are now banned by law in Oregon stores, but there are still thousands of flip-lids littering the landscape.

There are many who need to carry pills with them. Most small plastic drug containers crack and sometimes the tops come off. But there is an excellent

Margie, ready for beachcombing hike to end of Siletz (Salishan) Spit in January. On this day there was almost no wind, high overcast sky. Temperature was in low 40's. In the sack were gloves and lunch.

container that many have not yet discovered. Ask any 35mm camera user to let you have the plastic tube the film comes in. These Kodak brand canisters are small, have tops that are airtight and they will not come off accidentally. They are also waterproof. No one has ever been known to break one even if it was in a pocket and the fellow fell on it. These plastic film holders will not break when dropped and can be labeled with a felt pen. As pill holders, or for keeping matches dry, the authors have found nothing better.

ANIMALS OF THE SEASHORE

Many animals and birds frequent Northwest Coast beaches and some live there. Deer are common and on occasion, one might spot a bear. Overhead may be eagles and osprey. In areas where there are a lot of seagulls, it may pay one to wear a hat!

It is rare, but it does happen that a sea lion or sea otter may become stranded on a beach. Keep a good distance—they bite! Some jellyfish sting. These masses are also slippery to walk on, even with shoes. (Note: Although *Velella* look a lot like jellyfish they are not jellyfish and *Velella* do not sting. *See:* Chapter 6 and NOTES for Chapter 6.)

Beachcombers frequently happen upon clusters of strange sea life seen clinging to rocks. Strange as it may seem to some, the beautiful green, purple, orange "floral" arrangements are animals! These animals are the "non-food invertebrates"—intertidal life.

Starfish, sea urchins, sea cucumbers, mussels, barnacles, chitons, turban snails, and coelenterates are among the myriad species of animals in Oregon's intertidal areas. These strange creatures, which cling tenaciously to rocks in spite of tide and surf, form a source of pleasure to amateur biologists, and are used in professional studies by scientists. It is wise to know of harvest regulations pertaining to these tide pool and rock inhabitants before prying any off rocks. It is unlawful to poke at them, or to injure them. Some may be taken for personal use but bag limits change from time to time so are not quoted here. Collecting for scientific purposes, including weekend foraging for star fish for school classroom study, generally requires a written permit to be in the collector's hands at the time intertidal animals are taken. (Apply in advance at Marine Science Center, Newport, Oregon 97365.)

Deer at Ecola State Park, Cannon Beach.

DEER XING

FOR

WHALE WAS PROPELLER VICTIM

Forty-foot gray whale washed onto the beach near Cape Meares was victim of a large boat's propeller, according to a spokesman from Marine Science Center, Newport. Gray whales travel between Baja and the Bering Sea and are often seen along the Northwest Coast. Whale pictured is a "baleen whale," one that has no true teeth but has straw-like filter teeth for bottom feeding. The whale was buried on the beach after a bull-dozer spent several hours digging a hole.

CONSIDER THESE MATTERS:

Have a First Aid kit in the car. Carry a blanket in the car to wrap a shock victim, or to construct an emergency stretcher. Take bare-essential first aid items in a pocket on beach hikes: Band-aids, ace-bandage, clean handerchiefs. Bee sting kit. Small, sharp pocket knife.

For emergency flotation (life ring), use your spare tire wheel and all. If it has normal air pressure, it will float. Have a flashlight with at least two, size "D" cells. Take it on any beach hike that might last until dark.

ON NOVEMBER 17, 1977, a herd of about 14 elk romped down Broadway in Seaside, crossed a creek then headed for the beach.

Always:
REMOVE YOUR IGNITION KEY & LOCK ALL CAR DOORS

Keep a tool box with selected tools to make emergency vehicle repairs; tent repairs (upholster's needle and waxed thread); and patching material for leaky air matts. Carry spare flashlight bulbs in Kodak 35mm film capsules in the tool box. Electrical tape does wonders for non-electrical problems, but a roll of two-inch book binder's cloth tape, or mechanic's "aluminum" tape will nearly hold an automobile together if needed.

When snuffing out a camp fire or disposing of used charcoal from a cookout, *never bury the coals in the sand.* Undersand fires are common and the next person along could step on the coals resulting in severe burn.

Carry a sewing kit with buttons, safety pins, paperclips, rubber bands, and "Scotch" tape. Have a rucksack and fifty feet of nylon cord. (If beachcombers/hikers do not know how to tie knots, look in a Boy Scout handbook.

Take some gloves. Be the weather wet or dry, the use of gloves can save a lot of discomfort. Redwood splinters fester quickly and there is a lot of Redwood driftwood around the Oregon/California line.

Carry a walking stick! Choose a piece of driftwood that easily fits the hand, is about two inches diameter and at least elbow-high long. Such a stick can be used as a prod to test logs before stepping on them. The walking stick might also serve as a pry-bar. One might move some logs for his own safety as well as for the less-wary who are apt to follow.

Seasoned beachcombers and explorers everywhere make sure their tetanous inoculation is up to date before undertaking trips of adventure. There are sometimes huge sections of old docks often with jagged ends of metal and rusting nails on the beach. When the dock from the Mail Boat enterprise on the Rogue River was ripped loose during a flood, the dock went sailing out to sea. Beachcombers found it crumpled on the beach a few days later.

In camp a large sheet of plastic, rather than old-fashioned heavy tarpaulin,

King Neptune's hocky stick? Here is a section of rail from the once famous Bayocean railroad beachcombed during expedition specifically looking for evidence of the railroad.

will keep things dry when the weather changes. Include several terry-cloth towels. White is best because when dirty the soil is easier to see than on colored towels.

Some hikers wear a whistle on a cord around their necks. A whistle is more likely to be heard than a yell above the noise of the surf.

If the beachcombing is confined to the areas covered in this book, there will be no need for a compass, as the predominant lay of the beaches is north-south. A "pedometer" will indicate how far one walks. Be aware that most low cost pedometers, as advertised in popular magazines, have little or no guarantee. In the authors' experience few watchmakers will touch them for to overhaul one is more costly than replacing it.

It is foolhardy to turn inland from a beach and try to cross miles of underbrush trying to reach a road. If in difficulty, stay on the beach well back of the tideline where a downed person has a chance of being seen. One who falls beneath the underbrush in a wilderness between beach and highway cannot be seen from the air.

Persons who spend most of the year at home or at a desk job, may be more subject to sunstroke and sunburn than those who are in the elements continuously. Persons need to know their limitations before over-exposure or overexertion forces them down.

A teen-age girl once boasted, "When it comes to choosing a date for a hiking trip I'll skip the husky, bronzed, high-point fellow on the football team for a Scout. A Scout should be able to find something edible, build a fire, find directions by the stars and is taught first aid. Besides—he probably wouldn't get lost in the first place."

Beachcombing hikers can learn the same skills. Information about manuals and training guides is available from local Red Cross and Scout Council offices. The Red Cross and the Y.M.C.A. offers classes in First Aid, lifesaving and "CPR" (Cardio-Pulmonary Resuscitation). □

Last house in resort community of Bayocean Park poised for its crash into the sea on February 15, 1960. Of approximately 60 homes and summer cottages, only five were moved before final washout disintregated peninsula.

A short, agate-laden beach accessible only at low tide is open to beachcombers on Bayocean Spit near Cape Meares. Dale Webber stands on remains of concrete driveway which led to row of homes. Most homes fell into the sea when King Neptune wanted his sand back.

CHAPTER 16

KING NEPTUNE WANTS HIS SAND BACK

Coastal erosion can wreck a beachcomber's favorite spot or erosion can be a blessing, depending on what one is beachcombing for. If a fellow watched his house fall into the sea because the breakers collapsed the dune the building was sitting on, that might make one think a bit as to why he built on sand to start with. On the other hand, when something rare and desirable is uncovered because of erosion, it opens possibilities for research into the past some beachcombers may not have dreamed about.

In particular areas of the Northwest Coast there have been (and continues to be) annual winter problems with erosion. Along the Wasington coast in the area between Grayland and Tokeland, hundreds of acres have fallen prey to King Neptune and his pounding surf. Houses, schools, a Coast Guard Lighthouse, public highways, have been lost. Near North Cove, there was once a project where nearly eight hundred feet of shore line was to be stabilized by placing one hundred and fifty car and trunk bodies. These wrecks were then covered with heavy rock. But most of the rock washed out in less than three seasons and many of the car bodies and engine blocks were tossed about like toys once King Neptune decided he wanted his sand back. These locations are in one of the prime areas along the Northwest Coast for the beaching of glass floats.

Geologists acknowlege that one of the largest washouts along the Northwest Coast was on Tillamook (Bayocean) Spit, Oregon. Where once there was a beach over four miles long and football field-length wide, there is now just a few yards of rock at high tide. But the remains of the flat sandy beach can be beachcombed at very low tides. Tillamook County beaches are rich in agates and in history.

During the winter of 1972-1973 when the authors were researching for the book, *What Happened At Bayocean—Is Salishan Next?*, we were searching most closely for the remains of the Bayocean Railroad. This was a special, very narrow gauge line initially used to haul rock and sand for construction of the paved streets and building foundations. Later, the line was used to haul tourists on joy rides. Data about the railroad was fragmented and the research waters muddied by conflicting recollections of several old timers. We set out on a very low-tide-day to see what evidence, if any, we might discover to prove or disprove that there had indeed been a private rail line there.

We were not long in our search. Just under the crystal clear and very still water at the low tide line, was the rusted end of a length of rail protruding from the sand. After a cry of assistance and the arrival of help, the rail was pulled free. This piece was about fifteen feet long. Soon other lengths were found as well as parts from a bathtub, stove, and a head piece from a brass bed. We called it low tide-beachcombing-with-a-purpose.

Another instance when the results of sand removal by the waves—erosion—was observed at first hand occurred a few days after Thanksgiving Day, 1972. The authors were beachcombing, when we came upon two automobile tires wedged into the sand. Some metal was attached to them. Nothing would budge to our prodding. We walked on then left for the day. Returning to the same spot nearly one month later, during the big tide of December 20, we stood before a completely sand-free, front-end assembly from what appeared to be a Model A Ford. There were the tires—Ward's Riverside, size 6.00 x 16. The tie-bars and other parts were intact. One of the tires still held air. A gentle nudge sent the relic rolling a few feet. The tide had moved several feet of sand at this spot in about thirty days. □

Relic of town of Bay-ocean.

116

Driftwood and agate collectors will have a field day at Agate Beach State Wayside which is noted for large deposits of driftwood and agates.

CHAPTER 17

ROCKHOUNDING ON THE NORTHWEST COAST

Rockhounds get in their beachcombing too. And like the followers of driftwood or glass floats, weather does not stop them. But the tide the rockhounds seek is opposite to that wanted by glass float enthusiats. And if there is no wind — so much the better. On a low tide day recently, the weather on the beach was so thick the hundreds of stone seekers were bumping into each other as they slowly walked along, bent over at the waist, eyes darting from pebble to pebble through the fog.

Authority Clyde L. Browning, writing for *Lapidary Journal,* establishes that the stormy weather of the winter months exposes the best stone. He points out that the heavy tides, along with high winds, scours the surface sand from gravel beds leaving the beds exposes. Very low tides seem to bring forth two kinds of beachcombers: Rockhounds and clam diggers.

It has been claimed that there are more rockhounds on the beaches than beachcombers for glass floats and driftwood put together. There are millions of man-made glass floats in the sea, but how many agates are there? Browning insists that collectors of agates will never deplete the supply. Wherever there is ryolite rock and basalt containing agate nodules, there should be agates on the beach. The gem stones were formed millions of years ago, probably during the formation of the coast range mountains. Agates are set free when agate-bearing rock breaks loose and falls into the sea. As the water splashes, tumbles and grinds away, the gems, being harder, work loose. There are also agate beds along streams and in deserts. Agates are found along some beaches ranging from the Strait of Juan de

Agate bed at Ophir
Safety Rest Area,
Southern Oregon Coast

Fuca to near Eureka. Because the force of the sea is so great, especially during winter storms, agates are spewed upon the beaches in great numbers. But the sea grabs them back too, possibly as the breaker that put them on the beach recedes — just as happens with glass floats.

Summer season agate hunting turns up some fair examples, but the summer is not when serious rockhounds hound the beaches.

Beachcombers must be constantly aware of possible foot injury. The admonition to wear shoes — leather boots no less — is constantly coming up. But agate hunters work at water's edge and sometimes, as the pebbles move along with the wavelets, it is necessary to go ankle deep. Since the agate scrounger is likely to get wet feet anyway, why wreck a pair of boots? Good quality tennis-type shoes will protect feet. Light weight canvas shoes also rinse easily and dry quickly.

There are half-a-dozen or so locations along the Northwest Coast locally called "agate" beach. But the waterfront of the community of Agate Beach, Oregon, a long established settlement with its own postoffice, is one of the more prolific producers of high quality stone. Although not commonly found, sagenit agates and bloodstones are around.

Agates predominate, on northwest beaches, but there are other stones. Petrified wood is highly sought and it can be found. There is jasper, serpentine and a grossularite garnet referred to as "Oregon jade." Oregon, according to one study, is away ahead of other coastal states for the production of these gem-quality, semi-precious stones. There are blue and white banded agates, flower jaspers, and rockhounds identify Tillamook County beaches as yielding unusually large examples. Additional types on the beaches include: Carnelian, Ribbon, Cloud, Moss and Rainbow. It is generally agreed that the most unique agate is the one called an "enhydro," which contains a drop of water in an air bubble within the stone.

There are reports of white and pink jade, as well as the traditional green in gravel beds from about fifty miles north of the Oregon/California line, on down into California.

One authority claims that jasper is an impure agate but, winked an

(Left) **Plain pebbles can be made attractive with acrylic paint.** (Right) **Rock set in driftwood becomes table favor.**

octogenarian displaying a sales basket full of beautifully polished stones, "Call 'em what you like—I think they're all pretty!"

Rockhounds with beach experience emphasize that seekers of agates need be aware that just because a given beach produced a nice lot of stone on a given day, it does not follow that one can return to the same spot a few days later and carry on where he left off. One never knows what a wave will bring with it or uncover. A gravel bed will be here today or gone tomorrow. Clyde Browning suggests that the Pacific Northwest Coast in winter is ranked as the highest source for agates in the western states other than in southwest deserts.

One can beachcomb these rocky treasures along the Oregon Coast:

NORTH OREGON COAST

In addition to agates, there are varieties of jaspers; petrified wood; and garnet (Oregon "jade,"). Miocene fossils are in the cliffs bordering the Tillamook-Bayocean road. Prized sagenitic agates, containing needle-like inclusions, and bloodstones can be beachcombed between Yachats and Heceta Head, especially near the mouths of Big, China, Cummings, Tenmile and Squaw Creeks. Miocene Epoch marine fossils, including shells and bones of sea lions and whales are in the cliffs at Beverly Beach State Park, a few miles north of Newport.

SOUTHERN OREGON COAST

Gem quality agates; jasper; petrified wood; serpentine; and garnet are distributed from Coos Bay region to the Southern Oregon border. Whiskey Run beach, north of Bandon, produces agatized myrtlewood; blue and green banded agates; and flower jasper. There is Oregon "jade" and serpentine in the gravel bars of the Rogue River and on the sandy beaches near Gold Beach. Ecocene and Miocene Epoch fossils are easily found in the cliffs at Cape Arago State Park (west of Coos Bay). There are Pliocene and Pleistocene Epoch fossils in the cliffs south of the Cape Blanco lighthouse. □

Miocene fossils, commonly found along the Oregon Coast, can be identified.

Typical scene along stormy Northwest Coast in winter. Storm sequence photographed at Bandon, January 1977. Jetties at mouth, Coquille River, offshore rocks and restless driftwood (top, left). (below and top to bottom next page) Camera is safely behind windshield of camper at base of South Jetty. King Neptune's fury witnessed by lone seagull as huge breaker attacks North Jetty.....roars along.....and along.....strikes South Jetty in front of camper..... rumbles along top of North Jetty finally spending itself in the Coquille River. Bottom view looking toward sea from base of North Jetty the following morning. Continuing winter storms cause continuing damage to jetties which are surveyed regularly by the U.S. Army Corps of Engineers.

CHAPTER 18

CLAM GUNNERS AND LOW TIDE

It is the clam digger's responsibility to become familiar with annually issued regulations of the State in which he wishes to take clams.

Clam digging is inexpensive fun and a popular sport that can easily be combined with a beachcombing and camping trip. It is an activity that can be carried on almost all of the year and persons of all ages can participate.

Along the shores of the coastal bays are (one or more) varieties of clams which include gaper, littleneck, cockle, butter, softshell and geoduck (gooy-duck). The geoduck is the oddest of all. They are hard to dig being as much as four feet deep in the sand or mud of a bay. A geoduck weighs between three and seven pounds and its neck measures up to eighteen inches long. Geoducks are mostly dug in Puget Sound waters but they are also found in Netarts Bay.

The most popular clam to dig is the Pacific razor clam (*siliqua patula*). This is a very meaty shellfish that can be dug from California to Alaska. Razor clams are most abundant on surf-pounded ocean beaches and the best digging is during low (minus) tide.

One can believe that clam digging is popular when it is realized that some half-million individuals make nearly 1.5 million digger trips to ocean beaches along the Northwest Coast, then take home well over thirteen million razor clams each year. Until recently, most clams were dug with bare hands but for easier and more productive digging, a "clam gun" (special shovel) is lawful.

In some areas, razor clams grow as large as six inches, but the public clamor for them seldom lets them reach full size. Clams grow rapidly which explains their ability to keep pace with the diggers.

Rapid movement is the razor clam's chief protection against man, and is necesary for existence in his ever-changing beach environment. A thin, stream-lined shell with flexible lacquer-like coating, combined with a powerful digging foot, enables the razor clam to submerge rapidly in soft sand. However, this ability is mostly nullified in hard-packed sand bars.

The clam's digging "foot," has a sharp, rigid tip. When the clam finds it needs to move, the foot extends into the sand and a series of muscles forces water into it which flares out the tip like the head of a nail. With this as an anchor, the clam pulls itself downward at a rate of up to two feet a minute. Speed and skill are essential if man is to have any digging success because a razor clam will out-distance his pursuer in fluid sand. Razor clams do not move horizontally.

Digging falls into two basic catagories. 1. Surf-digging which pays greatest results in spring and fall. 2. Dry-digging in summer. (Some beaches are closed to clamming in summer.) Clams are taken in the surf by a single scoop of the shovel then grasping the neck of the clam with one hand. Dry digging is more productive for inexperienced clammers. It does not require as much speed.

Razor clams reveal their location by leaving "shows" (holes) when they withdraw their necks. These clams can often be made to "show" by foot-stomping.

Dry-digging is done on hard sand at low tide when the beach is not standing in water. Scan the beach for dimples about the diameter of a pencil. These are the "show" holes. Razor clams are from twelve to eighteen inches below the surface.

Surf digging is the more exciting of the two methods and is done in shallow water. Tap the sand with the end of the shovel handle. When the clam has been disturbed, it will pull its neck into the sand leaving the tell-tale dimple which will fill very quickly with sand.

When the "show" is seen, aim the clam gun about three inches *to the ocean side* of the hole and push the shovel straight down into the sand. Move the shovel handle toward the beach and work it back and forth a couple of times with one hand, and run the other hand down the back of the shovel and under the blade. When the end of the blade is felt, pull the shovel out of the sand at the same time feel through the sand for the clam. *Do not pry back on the handle* attempting to retrieve the clam on the shovel. Keep the blade nearly vertical to avoid hitting and damaging the clam.

Clamming scenes along the Washington Coast.

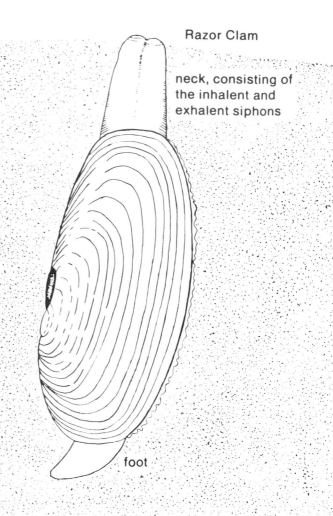

Razor Clam

neck, consisting of the inhalent and exhalent siphons

foot

Only one edge of the razor clam is sharp. Cut fingers can be avoided by always inserting the shovel into the sand on the side of the "show" *toward the ocean,* because razor clams are always oriented in the sand with the hinge (dull side) of the shell facing the ocean.

Razor clamming has been called a true sport for it is indeed a race with the clam. Digging other (bay) varieties—sometimes with a garden rake since bay clams just lie there—lacks spirit, claim many veteran "clam gun" artists.

It is lawful to use hands or "clam gun" (shovel) if hand operated, and to employ a cylindrical can or tube. Each digger must have a separate container, but need not have a separate digging device. *It is unlawful* for any person taking razor clams to replant them regardless of size or condition. All clams dug must be kept and applied to the bag limit for the day. *It is unlawful* for anyone to dig another's limit for him. *It is unlawful* to drive motor vehicles on a clam bed.

CLEANING RAZOR CLAMS

Just about everyone who ever ate a bowl of chowder made from fresh clams sees "stars" when they crunch on the sand. Some think that to have sand in the clams is their guarantee that the clams are indeed fresh. But is the "crunch" really necessary for fresh chowder?

Clams will purge themselves of their sand if they are given a chance. There are two methods. The first: Place one cup of corn meal and one cup of salt per gallon of water in a bucket or large pot. Leave the clams in this solution overnight and the clams will pump themselves clean. *Do not* leave clams in this solution for more than thirty-six hours. Remove the clams one at a time from the pot, rinse under fresh water, then drop them into a pot of boiling water for a few minutes. The second method is to put the clams into a burlap bag or in a wire basket. Hang the bag in still bay water from a dock or boat for twelve to eighteen hours. The clams will pump themselves clean. Many find the corn meal method more efficient and faster.

Cleaning clams is not messy and not difficult. The object is to remove the dark parts—the digestive tract and the gills. After snipping off the tip of the neck with scissors or very sharp knife, open the body from the base of the foot to the tip of the siphon. Observe the paired gills and palps. Take these out. Squeeze the digger (foot) then make a circular cut to remove the gut. Next, slit the digger so it will lie flat. Observe the small amount of intestine that extends through the foot, which is also to come out. Rinse the cleaned meat. You now have a fresh clam steak ready for cooking.

State parks and most motels along the clamming beaches have "clam laundro-mats" (a plank table with a water faucet) where cleaning can be done. Many young people who live near the beaches earn money cleaning clams for "city folk."

Getting clams home can be a problem for those who live a considerable distance. An easy way is to leave them in their shells and store them in a wet burlap bag. Or, use a bucket that has been cleaned and rinsed, and emptied of water. Place the clams in the bucket then cover them with a wet burlap bag. Keep the bucket of clams out of sunlight. Clams with unbroken shells, if kept cool, will survive for up to four days. Clean them immediately on arriving home. If the clams are cleaned at the beach, pack them in ice as all seafoods spoil quickly in warm weather. □

Hand painted razor clam shell done in Elementary School at Seaside.

CHAPTER 19

FINDING AND PRESERVING SEASHELLS

Wherever the sea touches the land, there is a probability of finding seashells. And those who walk the beaches in search of treasures tossed up by the sea often pick up shells as well as glass floats and driftwood.

Shells found washed up onto the shore are the skeletons of creatures of the mollusk order and these shells are often damaged by any number of means. To find perfect shells, the collector must usually hunt for them underwater or on exposed sand bars. Many people are unaware that true shell collecting is not limited to the tide line along the beach where they gather these weatherbeaten specimens. The complaints of never finding a glass fishing float are parallel with the complaints of never finding a complete (non-broken) shell. For either, one needs be at the right place at the right time. (*See:* Chapter 20.)

For a few days each month — during the full moon — the tide is low enough to bare far more of the beach than is usually seen. In some areas along the coast, sand bars only a short distance off shore are exposed. (One such bar is just off Bayocean Spit, Tilamook County, Oregon.) These normally underwater areas are where the mollusks live and breed.

Shell hunting on these low tide days requires the same amount of diligence as does glass float hunting on the high tides. Have clothing that is appropriate to the season. On the warm days a swimsuit, hat (there are birds up there!), and good shoes are basic. A lightweight knapsack with shoulder loops will free the hands from having to constantly carry anything. Many want to go barefooted on the wet sand but this is potentially dangerous because of the sharp cutting edges of shells that lie just under the surface.

If one steps into a boggy sand area, he might step right out of slipon shoes, therefore tie-on sneakers appear to be the best footwear. There is no equipment needed for shelling — just something to carry the treasures in at the end of the hunt.

Even for a small general collection, there are a few guidelines that shellers need to be aware of in order to create a fine exhibit. First, when collecting bivalves, one should remember that the many halves of shells on the beach are only "half" of the animals' house. Look for two halves joined with a hinge. Second, why show broken specimens when just a little more looking will probably turn up a perfect shell? Third, shells need to be properly cleaned — both inside and out. Techniques for shell cleaning will be discussed shortly. Another matter to consider for a display set of shells is the size of the shells. A larger than normal shell of a species, especially if it has good color and is perfect, increases the interest in the collection as well as its value.

When collecting bivalves, look for two shells joined with a hinge. Gastropods (right page) all grow in spirals. The fussy covering on the shell is the *periostracum*, which must usually be removed for positive identification.

Albino shells do turn up, according to seasoned shellers, and pure white shells are desired in a display set. Yet sometimes it is difficult to tell if the shell started life as an albino or lost its color in old age as some do. Any variation from the normal shape also makes a shell more desirable.

Skindiving and shelling now go hand-in-hand, for if perfect shells are wanted, the place to find them in underwater where they live.

To those who believe that all bivalves are clams and all univalves are snails, it could be a surprise to learn that there are thousands of named families of shells that have been found around the world. Our attention to shelling, being limited to the Northwest Coast, makes it a lot easier. Even so, there are many little shell groups that look almost identical along the Northwest Coastline. But each group has something unique about it thereby clearly defining the shell to a particular family. It requires a practiced eye to tell the difference. For the casual sheller, a good book at hand can make the difference between having an enjoyable or frustrating experience. The difference can be noted only on very close examination and comparison. The best guide the authors have seen is the all-color illustrated book by James Seeley White, *Seashells of the Pacific Northwest* (Binfords & Mort 1976). The soft cover edition takes little room in a beachcombers packsack. It is the ability to classify shells that makes the hobby of shell collecting fascinating.

When the experts tell of thousands of families of shells, they do not mean that all of them are huge size by tropical standards. Indeed, it has been estimated that seventy-five per cent of the identified shells are less than *one inch long*. Some collectors scoop buckets of sand along the beach, take this home, and with a magnifying glass search for shells not otherwise seen.

The collecting of sea shells can be an exciting and rewarding beachcombing experience, but if the shells are carelessly or improperly treated they can become an unpleasant nuisance. Many collectors have had to discard shells which, if they had been properly prepared, could have become a part of a noteworthy collection.

A shell collection should include the name of the shell as well as the location

where it was found, and other particulars.

Sea shells commonly encountered by beachcombers fall into two scientific classes: *Pelecypoda* and *Gastropoda*. The former can be readily identified by the two halves (valves) joined by a ligament (hinge). Razor clams are in this class. The latter class forms most of the popular shells and includes the cowries, cones, augers, miters, olives, and others.

The shells of bivalves (*Pelecypoda*) and gastropods (*Gastropoda*) are formed by the mantle of the animal which secretes lime. The mantle is responsible for the laying down of pattern and coloration on the shell's surface.

Bivalves swim, burrow, or remain stationary for life. Free swimmers move through the water or along the ocean bottom by rapidly opening and closing the valves thereby ejecting water which propels them forward. The burrowers (razor clams), dig through the sand or mud with a "foot."

Gastropods all grow in a spiral manner. Originating from a small protoconch, the shells grow in a (generally) clockwise direction. Each coil of the shell is known as a whorl. The final whorl, commonly called the body whorl, terminates at the aperture (or mouth) of the shell. It is through the aperture that the animal emerges to move about.

Most gastropods and many bivalves are coated with a *periostracum*. This brownish organic coating, found on the outside of the shell, protects it from the acid qualities of sea water. The *periostracum* on some species, is extremely thick and fibrous and completely obscures the pattern of the underlying shell. If this *periostracum* is not removed, positive identification of the species may not be possible. Other species (miters, cymatiums, trochus shells) may have this transparent *periostracum* which permits the shell pattern to be seen. The removel of this coating is a matter of preference.

A feature found on many, but not all, gastropods is an *operculum*. This is the horny (organic) or shelly (*calcareous*) "trap door" which the animal closes tightly within the aperture after retreating inside the shell. The "cat's eye" of turban shells is the *operculum* of that shell.

The mollusk, which inhabits gastropod shell, assumes the same shape as the shell since the animal coils within it. These mollusks extend foot, snout, eyes, and tentacles when active. Within the whorls of the shell are the internal organs. Because of the fragile nature of these organs, they are often difficult to completely remove unless care is taken. These organs, particularly the liver, easily decompose then give off a foul odor if not removed.

"AS FOUND" CONDITION OF SHELLS

Shells are found in these conditions: Alive; fresh-dead; dead; surf-rolled.

Serious collectors attempt to obtain shells found alive. An effort should always be made to keep live-taken shells alive until they can be treated. Fresh-dead shells are often hard to tell from live-taken shells.

Dead shells show obvious signs of deterioration. Frequently the aperture, normally polished, presents a dull green appearance which cannot be entirely removed by cleaning. If inhabited by a hermit crab, often the shell, particularly the lip, is broken or worn from being dragged over rocks or sand. Surf rolled shells are often damaged by the abrasive action of the sand. Usually nothing can be done to improve the appearance of "sanded" shells, but sometimes the application of a light film of mineral oil, or silicone grease restores some of their lustre.

After capture, placing the shells in a wet towel often keeps them alive for two or three days. Frequently, when kept in wet towels the animals expire in an extended position facilitating removal.

ANIMAL REMOVAL

Preparatory techniques are used to loosen the animal from the shell. Basically, there are two cleaning operations required before a shell is ready for display. The first is to remove the animal. The second is to clean the exterior of the shell. (It will be assumed that the animal is not to be kept.)

The two methods for loosening of tissue from shells are freezing or boiling.

Shells should first be throughly dried, then placed in a plastic carton with a tightly-fitting lid, or in a plastic bag. Metal containers, which are apt to rust, may cause discoloration. Leave the container in the freezer overnight. To thaw, *do not hasten the process* by placing the shells under running water or by putting them in an exceptionally warm place. Sudden expansion of the shell, when subjected to rapid temperature changes, may cause cracks. After the shells have thawed, wipe them with paper towels until all condensation is gone. Replace the shells in the

Mouth of Winchuck River, a few yards into Oregon at the California border.

container and return them to the freezer. Following this second freezing, remove them from the freezer and thaw as before. The soft parts should now be ready for removal.

Shells can be boiled to loosen the animal provided the boiling time is regulated to the relative size of the shell. Shells having a high external gloss should not be boiled as the high temperature frequently causes severe cracking of the finish. Boil in sea water since fresh water is a poison to sea shell occupants and causes them to retreat tightly into their shells, making removal difficult.

Place the shells in sea water at room temperature making certain that all portions of every shell are covered. Warm or boiling water is to be avoided as this causes the animals to tightly retract within the shell. Stainless steel is recommended as this will not discolor the shells. Place the container on a stove and bring slowly to a boil. Boiling causes the soft parts of the shell to contract and to firm up much the same way boiling an egg causes it to harden. Insufficient boiling time does not permit this to occur. Over-boiling, in addition to causing shell damage, allows the soft parts to become excessively hard. When too hard, the coiled part of the animal will probably break when an attempt is made to remove it. Merely bringing the water to a boil is sufficient for small shells. Bivalves and limpets may be treated by merely heating the water to a point where muscular attachment is destroyed. Experience is the best guide to the "cooking" time for a particular size and species.

Boiled shells must be cooled naturally. When the shells can be removed from the water by hand, the soft parts are ready for extracting. Take out these parts while the shell is still warm as delaying allows the animal to firm thereby increasing the risk of breaking off parts within the shell. For this reason, process only a few shells at a time.

Only shells of a similar size should be treated together. Also, fragile shells

Unique shape
of oyster shells
make
them
highly sought
by artists

should not be unduly agitated by the boiling water.

No method of animal removal is foolproof but when properly and promptly done, it need not be messy. The animal may be removed from the shell by flushing with water, uncoiling, hanging or decomposition. Remove the animal from the shell as soon as practical following the preliminary freezing or boiling since if it starts to decompose, its removal may become more difficult. Saving several week's shells and removing them from the freezer for an afternoon cleaning session leads to confusion, a thorough job not done, and rotten shells which must be thrown out. Therefore, it is suggested that only a few shells be cleaned at a time.

An attempt should always be made to use the flushing or uncoiling technique (or both) before considering alternatives. If one of these fails, decomposition treatments will salvage the shell. The hanging technique is specialized and applicable to only certain species. Rotting, while not technical, is time consuming. This method requires an area away from flies, animals and human noses. Professionals have rotting trays, cheesecloth shields, and other paraphernalia for use in this process. Most beachcombers who happen upon a handful of attractive shells do not go to these alternative methods for preserving them.

Flushing is probably the easiest and most dependable method of animal removal and is commonly used on shells which have been frozen. Depending upon the type of shell, flushing should not be used on boiled shells until after the uncoiling method has been tried. To do so may cram the animal further into the shell making removal more difficult.

Flushing is squirting a jet of water into the shell so the animal will wash out. If properly done, removal is immediate. Fit a small bore non-adjustable (fireman's type) nozzle to a garden hose. If possible, use a plastic or hard rubber nozzle since a metal one might chip the shell.

Flushing should be done in a large container such as a bath tub. There are several reasons for this. First, the richochet of the spray from a shell can quickly shower one not only with water but also with bits of animal. Next, it is easier to observe the operation under water than through a haze of spray. Finally, animal remains may be recovered for examination to be sure that removal has been complete. If possible, the *operculum* should be removed prior to flushing. Change water whenever it becomes cloudly with animal residue.

While firmly holding the shell under water, direct the nozzle into the aperture so the jet enters and leaves on an oblique. Pointing the jet directly into the aperture usually crams the flesh into the shell. Shaking the shell makes removal easier.

Uncoiling the animal from the shell is usually done with shells that have been boiled and while the shell is still warm. The animal should be visible in the aperture if the shells have been properly boiled. After removing the *operculum,* hook a suitable tool into the firm foot of the animal and pull and twist slowly, uncoiling the animal from the shell. Although the animal diminishes in diameter near its end, it also becomes more fragile toward the end. Resist the temptation to use jerky motions for to do so will pull the animal apart within the shell.

Several items can be used as tools. Dissecting needles are common. A hook can be made from a piece of stiff wire. Barbed fishhooks bent to an "L" shape and mounted (eye end) into a handle work very well. Only a stiff implement should be used as flexible wire usually bends and allows the animal to slip off or cause damage to the lip of the shell. Often a simple nut pick will do an excellent job.

If the animals in several shells of a like size break, this suggests insufficient boiling. Most shells can be reboiled, however the possibility of getting a second hold once an animal is broken can be considered a challenge. As earlier mentioned, one way to release a stuck part is to shake the shell vigorously.

PRESERVATION (ALCOHOL) TECHNIQUE

The preservation techniques should only be used when the other methods cannot be used or have failed. Very small shells are best preserved, thus freezing or boiling them is unnecessary. Further, the use of alcohol is often warranted when neither freezing or boiling is practical. For the collector who must travel by public conveyance, it is probably best to soak the shells in alcohol as soon as possible then remove the tissue before carrying an otherwise aromatic package in public. (If animal preservation is a consideration, only the alcohol technique is recommended. As a general guide, shells smaller than one-half-inch should be treated in alcohol and no attempt made to remove the tissue.

Shells up to about one-inch may be treated in alcohol and the animal extricated only if the collector elects to do so.

Only plastic or glass containers with tightly-fitted lids should be used. Dry the shells and place them in the container using undiluted 40 per cent isopropyl alcohol, or 70 per cent ethyl alcohol. The strengths given are minimum. Alcohol should be fresh, or if used repeatedly it should be strained through fine-woven material. Sufficient alcohol must be available to completely cover the shells.

Seal the container to prevent evaporation. Do not shake, but invert the container several times to be sure the alcohol has displaced the air within the shells. If the level of the alcohol drops, add more alcohol. Minimum immersion time is seventy-two hours. Larger shells take longer. Over exposure will not harm smaller shells. Shells may be kept in alcohol almost indefinitely if they were alive or fresh dead when treatment started.

Shells containing bits of animal treated earlier by freezing or boiling, may also be treated in alcohol provided that they have not started to decompose. Partially decomposed shells should not be placed in alcohol as the decomposition products are acidic and may damage the shell.

If the animal is to be removed after treatment in alcohol, it should be done as soon as possible. Small shells should be thoroughly dried after soaking in alcohol and allowed to air until they become odor-free.

CLEANING SHELL EXTERIORS

Limpets, barnacles, tube worms, and the like often cause severe damage to the surface of the unprotected shell because they produce an acidic secretion which dissolves a small portion of the host shell. The removal of these parasites usually presents no problem, but the damage they cause to the shell is irreparable. Shells heavily encrusted with these parasites can seldom be made presentable.

A stiff wire brush is best for removal of common growths. Often an old toothbrush and soap will do. At times a pointed tool will be required. Boiling or freezing will kill mollusks which are stuck to the shell. Algae and dirt are often removed by a short soak in dishwashing detergent to which a little household bleach has been added. Other growths can be removed with various chemicals. The use of chemicals for cleaning shells can be dangerous and should not be undertaken by novices to the technique. A little mineral oil rubbed over the surface of shells will frequently enhance the finish. □

It is perhaps a more fortunate destiny
To have a taste for collecting shells
Than to be born a millionaire.
Robert Louis Stevenson, *Lay Morals*

James Seeley White, underwater beachcomber.

CHAPTER 20

UNDERWATER BEACHCOMBING

It is well established that those who want perfect seashells will have to go where the shelled-animals live to find them, for we have seen that shells tossed upon the beach by stormy waves are often broken. So too, seekers of trophies from wrecked ships might find retrievable remains on the beaches, but better souvenirs are to be had on the bottom of the sea.

"Underwater beachcombing" is becoming a new term for some scuba divers who explore and scrounge ocean or river bottoms. While "land" beachcombing can be done by most everyone, underwater searches can only be carried out by experienced divers. Often the ocean is too rough for safe diving, but the protected side of many spits offers underwater beachcombers fine opportunities to retrieve long lost treasures, as well as oddities. Likewise, estuaries are often hiding places where unique potpourri can be found. In addition, a hint into the past history of the nearby town might be suggested from the assorted "junque" retrieved. After all, have not people been dumping their trash into oceans and rivers since time began?

It will be recalled that glass fishing floats are occasionally found with a little water in them. As stated earlier, it is believed that pressure may force water into microscopic openings when the float is dragged to depths on fishing nets. While searching the depths, James Seeley White liberated a five-inch glass float from a

Floats with water in them are rare and the volume of water is usually small. Jim White retrieved this float, nearly full, while *underwater* beachcombing.

damaged and long lost crabpot. There is no way of knowing how many years the float was under water. The float is clear glass, without markings, and resembles others known to be of American manufacture. It is nearly full of water.

Jim White has surveyed parts of the bottoms of many rivers and estuaries. One day, while on the "bottom," he and his associates found what was left of an old shipwreck in Nehalem Bay near the town of Wheeler. They also discovered odd-looking bottles and brought some up. On another underwater beachcombing expedition, this time near the town of Nehalem, White found a "relic hole." He later wrote:

We slipped into our diving tanks and gliding down the slope into the channel we noted about fifteen feet of visibility. Little spurts of mud shot up as startled clams withdrew their necks. We came upon a jumble of logs and limbs which marked the edge of the channel. Into an eddy there were many bits of debris deposited. Beyond the limbs we broke into the clear and a peaceful riverbottom. It was not entirely smooth, though, for there were clumps of cylinders partly camouflaged with barnacles, but clearly bottles, partly buried in the mud. While some of these bottles were contemporary beer stubbies, others were unfamiliar. I picked up one, then signaled that I was going to the surface to look at it closely. Back at the boat, I rubbed the mud away. The bottle had raised, embossed letters that read, "Schuster's Malt Extract."

White placed the bottle in the boat then went below to continue the search. Old green fruit jars with curved glass lids were scattered about. Near a log he picked up a slender quart beer bottle with a "lightning" stopper and fine lettering, "Enterprise Brewing Co. S.F. Cal." Some "Van Schuyver & Co., Portland, Oregon" whiskey bottles were recovered as well as little bottles marked "Thomas A. Edison, Special Battery Oil." There was a jar marked "The Samson Battery N.2."

A little later he brought up a mast-light lens and a starboard light from a boat. Soon the divers came upon the hulk of a boat with the bow firmly buried in the mud. Then they found remains of other boats which seemed to be commercial fishing craft. In the mud White picked up a German brass horn of a size that could have been mouth-operated by the skipper of a small vessel to signal his movement. There was a kerosene lamp, a brass steam whistle, some propellers and the crumbling remains of a French Horn.

There were patent medicine bottles, one with embossing, "Celro-Kola Company, Portland." In looking over the potpourri from this underwater beachcombing trip it became evident that while some oldtime residents of the area preferred malt extract, others relied on celery and cola (containing cocaine) compound to cure all ills.

So here was the beginnings of a picture of Old Nehalem. The types of patent medicines used were determined by the collection of bottles. A preference for western whisky was evidenced by the San Francisco and Portland bottles. Obviously, someone had owned a battery operated wireless set because of the containers for battery oil, the battery jar and a ceramic box that once held a large dry cell. Logging and fishing were means of livelihood because a long falling saw was liberated from the deep. And there were the boats.

What to make of it? Jim White wrote, "We felt privileged, sort of humble at having been allowed to discover the 'relic hole.' It was almost like finding there really is a Santa Claus."

Nehalem Bay is not the only place where successful underwater beachcombing can be followed. But underwater treks are not for the inexperienced. □

CHAPTER 21

VICARIOUS BEACHCOMBING

Just as collectors of postage stamps do, beachcombers enjoy showing their treasures and swapping yarns about how they obtained them. Surely, if King Neptune tosses something onto a beach, it will not be long before someone comes along, picks it up, then later shows it off.

Well planned, high quality beachcombers festivals are now a part of the calendar at Seaside, Netarts-Oceanside-Cape Meares, and Brookings, Oregon. These comprehensive displays of "flotsam, jetsam, and then some," are open to all who want to show their collections and who will abide by the rules of the sponsors. Admission is charged to the public who throng to these events with great enthusiasm.

The Seaside Beachcombers Festival is traditionally on the weekend nearest George Washington's birthday. One month later, the Netarts-Oceanside-Cape Meares and Brookings festivals are staged with equal zeal and are attended in force by visitors from those parts of the coast. At Grayland, Washington, there is an annual show of driftwood.

Of the three Oregon festivals, the Netarts-Oceanside-Cape Meares is the oldest dating from 1960. Apparently it got its start when local people met to discuss their collections.

Near Seaside, on April 2, 1967, a potluck breakfast was held in Margaret Atherton's Cannon Beach home. This is just a few steps from another of the better glass float collecting beaches along the Northwest Coast. A portion of the day was given over to greeting Amos Wood, who autographed his newly published book, *Beachcombing for Japanese Glass Floats* (Binford & Mort, 1967). A couple of dozen people dropped by to swap tales, admire glass balls, and to do a little beachcombing on the warm, sunny, spring day. Actually, this was the fourth year the "Cannon Beach Bunch" had met to compare trophies from beach foraging. But the group was growing and it was becoming difficult to find a home large

Some beachcombers specialize in glass fishing floats, some driftwood. Here is a ribbon-winning display (left) of beachcombed bottles exhibited at Netarts-Oceanside-Cape Meares Beachcombers Festival. At right is award winning interpretative display at Seaside Beachcombers Festival which ties each float to place on map of North Pacific Ocean Rim where authors obtained the floats. Represented are floats from Washington, Oregon, Kwajalein, Roi-Namur, Ebeye, Guam, Tinian, Japan plus books cited in General References. *See* p. 178.

enough to hold them all. There was discussion about holding an organized late-winter festival where general beachcombed material would be displayed for public viewing. In addition, for those who could not walk the beaches, slide shows or movies of beachcombing might be offered. It was a grand idea. It proved to be the genesis of more than the planners envisioned.

At about this same time, the Seaside Chamber of Commerce became interested in bolstering winter-lulled motel and restaurant business. Seaside has been a resort community since 1870 and its people have seen all sorts of Chamber of Commerce tourist-attracting events. But there does not appear to be any record of a group ever sponsoring a convention of beachcombers! Although space for large gatherings in the Seaside-Cannon Beach area had always been a major stumbling block, the Seaside Boosters Club brainstormed the idea of having a weekend-long beachcombers festival. Many of the ideas of the Cannon Beach enthusiasts were incorporated into the Seaside objective. Committee members asked questions, obtained local merchant assistance, and ate potluck suppers while pondering problems. Then the volunteers knocked on doors of local beachcombers who were asked to haul out their treasures for public viewing. Some refused. Others cooperated. By year's end 1967, the committee felt it was ready to take the plunge. In February 1968, the First Seaside Beachcombers Festival sprawled its *potpourri* throughout the Seasider Hotel.

The Portland newspapers had announced the coming event and committee members had donated evenings for tacking up pennants and signs in neighboring towns. When the great weekend came, it rained! It poured! Wind blasted at signs and awning banners. Breakers crashed all along the beach. On the highway between Portland and Seaside cars slowed because of snow. But there is obviously no weather that will stop a true beachcomber, for by mid-Saturday Seaside was jammed with people beyond the wildest expectations.

The Chamber of Commerce was quick to realize they had a good thing going.

Committees were formed to continue sponsoring the festival which would be held every February. Dual chairmanships of the various areas of responsibility were created, thereby allowing one person to rotate out of a job ("and to get a little rest") each year. New blood entered from the town's populace. But something had to be done about a place to hold this festival and other business-building schemes which were looming on the horizon. The people of Seaside went to the polls and voted to build a Convention Center.

The Beachcombers Festival was the first event scheduled for the new auditorium—but would the building be ready in time? Contractors and their crews worked diligently. There were anxious days. But custodians and volunteers hauled out debris from the construction then mopped the floor right up to the moment of opening the door to waiting crowds.

Selected artisans in driftwood finishing and painting, seashell collectors and glass float specialists, are invited each year to exhibit and to explain their hobbies in scheduled demonstrations.

Area newspapers, radio and television stations, encouraged by the committee, provide advance announcements about the festival. In addition, comments by past visitors to friends spreads the word. As a result, the Seaside Beachcombers Festival draws thousands of admission-paying enthusiasts annually from hundreds of miles away (thus advance motel reservations are now required).

At first, only nearby beachcombers set up displays, but in recent years beachcombers who live great distances truck their treasures to the Convention

141

Margie, with string-of-pearl-shells found at Willapa Bay, Washington. Length is about five feet. Weight, 23 pounds. Bert (right) showing Okinawan burial urn beachcombed near Gold Beach, Oregon. Urn was exhibited at Brookings Beachcombers Festival.

Center. These objects include every known size, shape and color of glass floats; plastic and cork floats; metal floats; driftwood-large—unfinished; driftwood-large—finished; driftwood-small—unfinished; driftwood-small—finished; driftwood resembling animals; driftwood made into furniture; bottles; light bulbs from small home-use shapes to gallon jug-size colored globes from foreign night fishing operations; ship parts; wine and water casks; foreign beer kegs; always at least one ship's life ring; agates; seashells; remains of floating ordnance; barnacle encrusted objects; and whatever!

While most beachcombers display their collection for the pure fun of sharing and talking about their finds, others plan their displays months ahead in

Margie with her interpretation of Alexander Calder's fish mobile (*kinetic art*) which hangs in Smithsonian Museum. Each piece of beachcombed glass is suspended thus free to swing with air movement. Margie's mobile is a ribbon winner at Seaside and Brookings Beachcombers Festivals.

efforts to win blue ribbons. The judging is done by panels of seasoned beach-combers who have professional backgrounds in a host of fields. Anxiety runs high among these exhibitors who have the zeal of those inbued with the American spirit of competition. But everyone cannot win and not a year goes by without a challenge to a judge by one whose display did not take a ribbon.

Although many displays are in the same subject category and with the same basic materials, the exhibits will usually be quite different because of the creative genius of the designers. Beautiful mobiles, whose balances are created after many hours of painstaking trial and error, gyrate in the gentle drafts stirred by hundreds of fascinated viewers passing near them. In some festivals there is a salon of photography, the pictures all relating to beachcombing.

Some of those who demonstrate their skills of making art objects out of beachcombed materials sell their creations to enthusiastic bystanders.

Should a theme ever be found necessary for one of these festivals it might be, "Beachcombing is for everyone. Here is how to go about it. Let's compare notes."

The authors have observed that the majority of displaying-beachcombers prefer not to sell their collections. This is an about-face from most artists'

Root-ball was beachcombed near Brookings after floating down probably the Chetco or Winchuck River. Following decoration it was displayed at Brookings Beachcombers Festival.

exhibitions where the idea of the show is to sell the paintings. Nevertheless, there are plenty of hand-made, beach-related items for sale by the corps of demonstators who are on hand to show visitors how to do things. Traditionally, sale items include autographed copies of books on beachcombing by nationally published authors who are active Northwest Coast beachcombers. Some of these writers make their time available to the festival by presenting slide shows. These illustrated lectures not only deal with the Northwest Coast but sometimes discuss beachcombing in faraway places. These talks are repeated many times throughout the weekend often to standing-room-only throngs who alternate between the two projection rooms.

The scene is repeated at Netarts-Oceanside-Cape Meares and Brookings a few weeks later. There is a "Beachcombers Chamber of Commerce" made up of local people from the Netarts, Oceanside and Cape Meares communities who handle all of the details. Netarts and Oceanside are just two miles apart directly south of Cape Meares (west of Tillamook). Usually the annual festival alternates between the two villages of Netarts and Oceanside where fire engines are parked on the street and the fire halls become exhibit centers. The atmosphere in both communities is homey and one can buy a piece of home-made pie at the refreshment stand. Though on a much smaller scale, when measured by facilities and numbers of exhibitors, the enthusiasm in these Cape Meares towns is equal to that at Seaside and crowds of ticket-buying visitors swamp the narrow streets come beachcombers festival weekend.

At the Brookings Beachcombers Festival, the Brookings-Harbor Chamber of Commerce arranges for displays to be set up (usually) in the high school gym. A nearby classroom is provided for the slide shows. The Brookings Beachcombers Festival is the youngest of the three but crowds and enthusiasm have increased to a point where advance motel reservations should be made.

The displays at Seaside and Netarts-Oceanside-Cape Meares run heavily toward glass fishing floats and *potpourri*. At Brookings, where fewer floats are found and driftwood is more plentiful, the exhibits lean more toward wood.

In all three locations, Oregon State Parks and private campgrounds are nearby for the growing numbers of festival visitors who arrive in campers and do not depend on motels.

If one is unable to comb the beaches for himself, then the next best thing to do is to attend a beachcombers festival. The displays are imaginative and sometimes fresh-found objects (?) are brought into the auditoriums complete with sea-smells!

So far, all of these Oregon beachcomber festivals have been in ground-level halls thus wheelchair-bound "beachcombers" have easy access. □

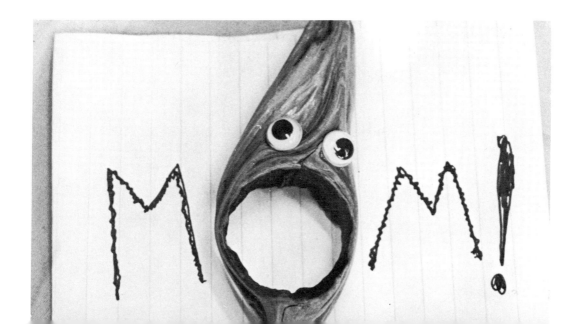

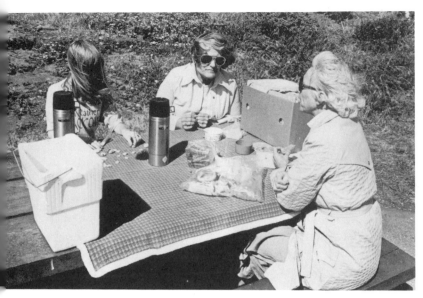

Ophir Safety Rest Area, South Oregon Coast. Although a sunny August day, wind was crisp dictating that food be protected from blowing sand. Margie (center) with visitors from South Carolina.

APPENDIX A

LET'S EAT AT THE BEACH

The question of where and what to eat while on a trip to the beach is often complicated because of a lack of suitable restaurants within a resonable distance of a campsite. Whether one is a tent camper, or uses a deluxe RV, some basic ideas on foods and how to prepare them is often valuable.

Probably the basic reason for going to the beach in the first place is to get away from home. This also includes getting away from kitchen chores. Accordingly, here are some suggestions with two ideas in mind. 1.) Food preparation in the camper without damaging the interior of a vehicle. 2.) Quality meals with a minimum of fuss to fix them.

At home, most modern kitchens have an exhaust fan over the stove. Most campers do not have fans and damage to the walls and ceiling of those without fans can result from frying or continuous boiling of foods. This is because the interiors of many moderately priced units are frequently finished with contact paper. The grease and steam treatment to the walls and ceilings resulting from heavy cooking on a propane stove in a confined space will eventually cause the contact paper to lift then fall off.

Grease on the walls, combined with contact paper-lift from boiling, wrecked the interior of a fifteen-foot travel trailer in which the authors had an interest within just *two camping seasons.*

In these food preparations, the "before trip" recommendations presume home refrigeration of up to about twenty-four hours. Foods prepared earlier and quick frozen will hold about twelve hours out of the freezer and could thaw by the time most people reach the beach for the first evening meal. Prepare meals to be entirely consumed — no leftovers.

Avoid carrying easily spoiled items, especially devilled eggs and sandwiches

"Suitcase kitchen." Electric hotplate, extension cord, table service, cocoa and tea. Motel operators frown on such "luggage" but carrying such lowers trip costs by eliminating many restaurant meals.

which contain mayonnaise unless a well iced chest is available.

Dish washing in camp is always bothersome. Try paper plates—but not for soup. If there are just "two for dinner," have a cozy time eating out of the pot!

The menus and methods offered here are the result of over twenty years camping by the writers and their family, plus elaborations on some ideas which were encountered while camping with the Boy Scouts.

★　　　★　　　★　　　★

1. BEACHCOMBERS MEAT STEW PACKETS

BEFORE TRIP:

Line a two-quart size sauce pan with two layers heavy duty foil. Cut foil long enough for ends to fold over to close top of packet. For best heating at the beach, packet should not be over two inches thick.

Remove fat and dice leftover roast chicken, turkey, beef, lamb, or pork along with bite-size carrots and celery. Place in foil. With a rubber spatula, so as not to damage foil, mix meat and vegetables. Spoon in leftover gravy. Sprinkle lightly with *au jus* powder of appropriate flavor. (Do not salt.) Add one-fourth teaspoon dried onion flakes if desired. Fold ends of foil to close packet and remove packet from pan. Place packet in plastic container same size as pan. Store in freezer or refrigerator until time of departure.

AT THE BEACH:

If cooking over open fire with grate: Transfer packet from plastic bucket and place on grate in area of low blaze or close to coals.

If cooking on a propane or gasoline camp stove: Turn contents of packet(s) into a two-quart sauce pan. Add water for desired consistency. Heat over low flame. Stir as needed.

Option: Add precooked small new potatoes (15 ounce can).

Serve with hard roll and finger salad of carrots, celery, radishes, sliced (raw) zucchini.

★　　　★　　　★　　　★

Basic lighting and cooking equipment for tent and vans and in covered pickup trucks. Some gasoline lanterns (shown) accept "regular" or white gasoline. Most stoves (shown) require white gas or brand-name fuel. Drum at rear is heater attachment for stove. Handy in tents on a cold morning. Matches must be protected from dampness on Northwest Coast.

2. TIDE'S - COMING - IN - HURRY - UP - CANNED SPAGHETTI

BEFORE TRIP:

Fry one-half pound lean hamburger, or cut up one-half pound wieners or bologna. Add one to one-half cups fresh sliced mushrooms. Canned (drained) mushrooms can be substituted. Sprinkle some salt and pepper. Consider adding a pinch of dried onion flakes. Pack in two thicknesses of heavy duty foil.

AT THE BEACH:

Empty can of spaghetti and all of the sauce into a two-quart sauce pan. Heat over outside fire or on camp stove. Stir to distribute heat. When very hot add meat from prefab packet and mix. For zesty flavor add several one-half inch cubes of Oregon cheddar cheese. When cheese is melted and has been lightly stirred in, serve with hard rolls or bread sticks, finger salad.

★　　★　　★　　★

3. PREFAB FAMILY SPAGHETTI POT

BEFORE TRIP:

Completely prepare a regular home style spaghetti dinner. When cold, pack for trip and refrigerate. Grate Oregon cheddar cheese and store separately in plastic sandwich bag. See directions for TIDE'S-COMING...SPAGHETTI but increase quantities as required. Or: completely prepare a usual home style spaghetti dinner. Pack in foil.

AT THE BEACH:

Warm in large sauce pan. When nearly ready, sprinkle with cheese. Serve with ripe pitted olives, hard rolls or bread sticks, finger salad.

★　　★　　★　　★

4. OPEN-FIRE BEACHCOMBERS SPAGHETTI POT
(Not recommended for in-camper cooking)

BEFORE TRIP:

See directions for TIDE'S-COMING...SPAGHETTI. Increase quantities as required. Prepare favorite sauce and store in covered plastic container.

Of the many cooking outfits available, authors chose stainless steel "nesting" set where everything fits within large pot at left.

AT THE BEACH:

Place large pot of water on grate over hot campfire. Time can be saved by starting with hot water from State Park restroom. Cover pot until water is in rolling boil. Cook dry spaghetti following usual home methods. Drain. Stir in sauce. Garnish with pitted olives, serve with Oregon cheddar cheese sticks, crisp rolls, dill or sweet pickles and finger salad.

★　　★　　★　　★

5. OPEN-FIRE MACARONI AND CHEDDAR

BEFORE TRIP:

Place desired number of servings of precooked macaroni and cheese into individual double-layer foil packets. While spooning into packets, place one-eighth- to one-quarter-inch slices of Oregon cheddar cheese in the center of each packet. Add dashes of paprika while spooning. Close packet carefully retaining double-layer foil on *all* surfaces. Store in freezer or refrigerator until departure.

AT THE BEACH:

If cooking over open fire with grate: Place foil packets on grate and turn frequently. May require about forty minutes to heat completely through and melt center slice of cheese. Side dish: Canned French style string beans. Remove paper label from can. Open can but leave the lid to float in open top. Pour off small quantity liquid. Place on grate where beans will boil in the can.

For cooking on a propane or gasoline camp stove: Empty the packets into a sauce pan as described in BEACHCOMBERS MEAT STEW PACKET.

Serve with crisp rolls, slices of Oregon cheddar cheese, finger salad.

★　　★　　★　　★

6. BLUSTERY-DAY CHILI FOR BEACHCOMBERS

AT THE BEACH:

Warm canned chili with beans in sauce pan on either a shielded open fire or on camp stove. If more meat desired, refer to before trip preparations for TIDE'S COMING...SPAGHETTI. If "chili bowl" (soupy) style desired, add up to three-fourth can water. Optional: Stir in pitted ripe olives. Just before serving, garnish with tuft of fresh alfalfa sprouts. Serve with crackers, salad.

Individual "canned" lunches are easy to carry in pack or pocket. In Oregon, flip-top beverage cans are illegal and deposit is required on all pop and beer cans and bottles.

NOTE: Before using a canned chili at the beach, experiment at home as some brands are more soupy (watery?) than others. *See:* instructions for alfalfa sprouts following Menu No. 12.

★　　★　　★　　★

7. LOW-TIDE EXTRA-CLAMMY CHOWDER

AT THE BEACH:

Warm over either campfire or on camp stove following packer's instructions on label. Add one 8-ounce can of chopped clams with nectar for each 15-ounce can of condensed chowder.

Serve in large bowls. Float one-half pat of butter or margarine just before serving. Optional: Just before serving add tuft of fresh alfalfa sprouts. Offer hard roll or crackers, finger salad.

★　　★　　★　　★

8. BEACHCOMBERS OPEN-FIRE FOIL DINNER

BEFORE TRIP:

Prepare individual packets. While most menus consider very lean hamburger (ten per cent fat), the foil dinner requires the twenty-thirty per cent variety for moisture and to prevent severe sticking while cooking. Use two thicknesses heavy duty foil.

Allow one-fourth- to one-half-pound hamburger per packet. Build as follows: In the center of the foil, place uncooked meat patty. Add dash of selected seasonings including steak sauce and dried onion flakes, salt and pepper. Place several layers of *thinly* sliced raw carrot. Pile on one or more layers of one-half-inch thick sliced raw potato. Options: Add celery, mushrooms, green peppers, catsup, or three-fourth-inch thick slice beefsteak tomato.

Carefully fold the foil over the food to seal the packet.

AT THE BEACH:

This foil dinner is intended to be cooked directly on coals of campfire. Be careful not to puncture packet when shoving it around. Allow one hour on good coals for thorough cooking. The steam in the packet will lightly cook the vegetables.

★　　★　　★　　★

Of several brands of cheddar cheese manufactured on the Oregon Coast these shown have wide appeal for type, flavor, quality. Tillamook and Bandons cheeseries have viewing galleries.

9. OREGON CHEDDAR GRILL

While a skillet is preheating on medium (propane), or on campfire grate, spread butter or soft margarine on two slices of bread. Place one slice of bread butter-side-*down* in the pan. Carefully lay slices of Oregon cheddar cheese on the bread. For an easy melt, cheese slice should not be over three-sixteenth-inch thick. Put second piece of bread, butter-side-*up,* on top of the cheese. With pancake flipper, turn sandwich several times until both surfaces are golden brown and cheese becomes "squishy" to the touch.

Serve with sweet or dill pickles, green or ripe olives, celery, carrot sticks, sliced zucchini (and beer if you like it).

★　　★　　★　　★

Crab–cheddar melt. It you brought your sandwich toaster to the beach, brown English muffin halfs then pile on fresh crab meat (or shrimp) plus thin sliced Oregon cheddar cheese. Leave in toaster until cheese melts through meat. Top with fresh alfalfa sprouts.

10. BEACH PATROL S.O.S.

BEFORE TRIP:

Fry hamburger and pour off grease. While cooking, chop the meat into fine crumbles. Add salt and pepper, dash of dried onion chips. Package in foil formed to fit into bottom of sauce pan to be used in camp. Freeze or refrigerate meat until trip.

AT THE BEACH:

Open can of condensed cream of mushroom soup and pour into sauce pan. Add one-half can water or skim milk. Heat over low fire. When steaming but not boiling, open hamburger pack whether frozen or thawed and put meat block into sauce. Cover pan and warm contents thoroughly. Serve in soup bowl with crackers or bread sticks or on instant mashed potatoes.
Side dish: Cold (canned) pickled beets.　　Salad: Sliced raw zucchini and carrot sticks.

11. BEACHCOMBERS BOILED BUCKET BANQUET

When a camping family is stuck inside a tent on a rainy day and all seems lost as to how to prepare a hot, delicious, meal—especially if there are little ones under foot—and it is neither practical nor safe to put a cookstove inside the tent; believe it, there is a solution!

This dinner can be expanded or diminished depending on the numbers and sizes of appetites to be satisfied. The basis is meat and two vegetables.

Start a fire in a camp grate with some of the dry wood that you kept dry by tossing it under the car at the first sign of rain. A wet canvas "lean to" or a "sky cloth" on a rope, will protect the sputtering fire until it gets roaring.

While the fire is getting started, fill a ten-quart bucket to the three-fourths-full mark with water--hot if available from a campsite utility building. As soon as the fire is reasonaly high, place the bucket on the grate. (Experienced campers carry a piece of tin to sandwich between the grate and the bucket.)

As soon as the water is boiling, carefully drop these canned foods into the bucket.

1 One-pound canned ham (remove key from bottom of can but don't lose the key!)
1 One-pound canned cut green beans
1 One-pound canned cob-cut corn, or Mexi-corn or white shoepeg corn
1 Six-ounce canned pineapple
1 canned Boston brown bread.

When water has returned to full boil if fire seems too hot, move bucket with pair of lock-grip pliers to side of grate. *(Water in bucket is scalding, heavy, and moving it is an adult chore and should not be left to anxious-to-help youngsters.)* If boil stops, add small size firewood, or move bucket directly over blaze.

Allow full hour for boiling water to thoroughly heat food.

When heating time is completed, remove bucket from grate. The slightly puffed cans can be taken from the water with tongs or pliers. Place a rag, or thickness of paper towel, on top of each can to take up squirt of steam or juice when can is punctured. Pour off all liquids except from the pineapple.

Serve on double thicknesses of paperplates: Hot slices of ham covered with pineapple slices. Add one teaspoon of brown sugar to the top of the entree. Spoon a little pineapple juice over the sugar. Place servings of beans and corn alongside ham. Top corn with pat of butter, or margarine, and dash of salt and pepper. Since it's a cool, rainy day, serve with hot apple or tomato juice.

The hot brown bread, served with butter and honey, might become dessert.

This is a great meal with a happy ending because there are no dishes, pots, or pans to wash!

12. PACIFIC FISH OPEN-FIRE STEWPOT (serves 8-10)

One-half pound diced bacon (optional)
One-half-cup chopped onion, or one tablespoon dehydrated onion flakes
Two cups celery cut into one-inch lengths
One-half lemon, thinly sliced or two tablespoons of reconstituted juice
One quart water (preheat)
Two No. 2½ cans tomatoes with juice (5 cups)
One-fourth-cup catsup
One-fourth teaspoon curry powder
Two teaspoons salt
One tablespoon Worcestershire sauce
One-eighth-teaspoon Tabasco sauce
One-and-one-half-pound Oregon raw shrimp, cleaned and deveined
One pound fish (red snapper, ling cod or sable fish)
Two-thirds-cup Sherry wine (optional)
Four tablespoons butter
One pound scallops (optional)

Saute bacon in skillet until golden brown. When done, place in large kettle on grate over roaring campfire. Add onion, celery and cook for five minutes stirring constantly. Add lemon slices (or juice), very hot water, tomatoes, catsup, curry powder, salt, Worcestershire and Tabasco sauce. Cook slowly for thirty minutes. Do not add fish until batch is extremely hot so fish will cook quickly. If scallops are large, cut in half. Add scallops, fish, shrimp, wine and butter. Cook just a few minutes until fish flakes easily with fork.

Serve in soup bowls.

Touch off with carrot sticks, sliced zucchini, radishes. Augment with bread sticks, crackers, or hard rolls.

★   ★   ★   ★

SALAD GREENS (Alfalfa Sprouts)

When a family is camping for a considerable time, the matter of obtaining fresh salad greens comes up. Although many have discovered alfalfa sprouts, most people have apparently not learned how to grow their own. To grow sprouts requires only a one-quart jar (wide-mouth is best) preferably with a strainer or cheesecloth for a lid. This campsite "farming" does not rob valuable beachcombing time.

The flavor of alfalfa sprouts purchased in grocery store bags can be considerably improved, if

"Hairy Bull" or "fuzz" sandwich. On wheat bread build with thick slides of bologna and Oregon cheddar cheese. Spread mustard, relish, top with sprouts.

one does not want to start from scratch. Place the pale sprouts from the store bag in the one-quart jar. Fill the jar with cold water. Shake well, but not vigorously, to "water" every seedling in the jar. Pour off the water until a few drops remain. Close the jar and place the jar of sprouts in the sun. Within hours the sprouts will start greening up. With the greening comes more flavor. Rinse and drain unused sprouts once each morning and evening to keep them fresh. Alfalfa sprouts are continually growing until eaten.

TO GROW SPROUTS FROM SCRATCH: Obtain seeds from a health food store. Place just enough seeds in the bottom of a one-quart wide mouth jar to barely cover the bottom. Add about two cups of cold water. Let the seeds soak for about eight hours. At the end of the period, drain, then place the jar in a warm, dark place. During summer camping, a warm, dark, place can be created by putting the jar of damp seeds into several thicknesses of brown *paper bags*. (Never use plastic—the loss of air will rot your "farm".) Set the tightly closed bags in the sun. Once each morning and evening rinse the seed with cool water and immediately return the jar to the bags. In about three days, the sprouts should be over one-inch long and pale. From this point, handle as instructed for a store packet of sprouts for greening.

Note that the hulls from the seeds float to the top of the jar while the sprouts are being rinsed. Some people prefer to eat these (dried) hulls as bran, and some just leave the bran with the sprouts. Others may want to pour off the bran with the rinse water.

SUNSHINE TEA

Beachcombing campers can make their own tea on the scene without a fire.

TEA FOR 2:

Fill a one-quart jar with cool water. Float 2 tea bags, preferably Orange Pekoe and Pekoe Cut Black Tea, in the top of the jar leaving the tags on the outside. Placing a cover on the jar will keep the bugs out, but whether there is a lid or not does not appear to have any bearing on the infusion process for brewing tea.

Set the jar in the sun and leave it alone for about two hours. Allow a little longer on overcast days. On a fair-weather day, the temperature of the water in the jar may rise to about 90 degrees F. or higher, even though the weather is considerably cooler.

When one observes the brew to be rich in color yet crystal clear, the tea is ready for drinking. The tea can be cooled in a tub of sea water, or if ice is available, add some for ice tea.

For a larger quanitity, use a well-washed wide-mouth 1-gallon size pickle jar and 9 tea bags. The infusion time is a little longer, When the brew is rich in color, it is ready.

Large jars of Sunshine Tea can be chilled overnight in a refrigerator down to the usual 39 degrees refrigerator temperature. Serve without ice to avoid diluting the flavor. For the ice-we-must-have visitors, prehandle by freezing tea in an ice cube tray. □

Fill quart jar with cold water and place in sunlight. About two hours later tea is deep in color yet crystal clear.

Persons without Reservations wait in line hoping for cancellations or no-shows at Fort Stevens State Park.

APPENDIX B

NORTHWEST COAST CAMPGROUNDS

PUBLIC AND PRIVATELY OWNED FACILITIES

PUBLIC OWNED:

Abvr. used in this list: SP, State Park; CP, County Park; FS, National Forest Park; NP, National Park; SF, State Forestry Dept. Park; MP, Municipal (city) Park; W, Winter—open all year; R, Reservation recommended.

Compass directions: n, north; e, east; s, south; w, west.

(#), accomodates either trailers or tents. Watch for trailer length limits as many trailer spaces will *not* accomodate 5th wheelers.

RV column in chart is for Recreational Vehicles, Travel Trailers, Campers.

Most State Parks along the Northwest Coast are open all year for picnicking during daylight hours. In Washington, few Safety Rest Areas and State Parks offer hot water except in overnight parks where there are coin-operated showers. In Oregon almost all Safety Rest Areas and State Parks offer hot water, but in overnight camping parks, hot water hours are posted in the showers which, at this writing, is free. Wood for campfires is free only in a few parks. Camps where there is a charge for firewood are posted. (Those planning on using a camp fire should provide their own kindling carried from home as much wood in the camps are chunks from fallen trees, or large scrap from nearby timber operations.) In Oregon the most popular overnight parks operate a reservation (R) system during summer. A percentage of spaces is kept for drive-in campers, but one should not depend on being accomodated on this "chance" basis. If turned away—what next? It could prove to be a poor decision to merely park alongside a road for a night due to limited side clearance and highway regulations. Reservations can be made on toll-free telephone from any within-Oregon point (during summer) to a central booking office, or at the check-in office of all State Parks offering overnight campsites. A small fee is charged for the (R) service. Conveniently spaced overnight

camp facilities are open in winter (W) along the Oregon coast.

Daily newspapers from local or nearby cities are generally available from coin-operated machines at rest rooms in the overnight parks.

Read the Park Regulations (posted near rest rooms) as to use of radios, amplified musical intruments, control of pets, disposal of trash and waste water.

The numbers of campsites and names of parks that are in operation change from year to year. In recent years, environmental considerations have caused entire parks to close without notice due to temporary problems with fresh water supply or sanitary conditions. Before making a trip into any area, check with area park headquarters.

WASHINGTON

NAME OF PARK	TYPE	TENT SPACES	RV SPACES	NEAREST TOWN
Bogachiel	(SP)	44	(#)	(s) Forks
Mora	(NP)	91	(#)	(w) Forks
Klahaie	(FS)	18	4	(nw) Forks
Kalaloch	(NP)	195	(#)	Kalaloch
Queets	(NP)	12	0	Queets
Olallie	(FS)	14	(#)	(sw) Quinault
Willaby	(FS)	7	12	(sw) Quinault
Falls Creek	(FS)	5	21	(ne) Quinault
Pacific Beach*	(SP)	(#)	125	in Pacific City on beach
Ocean City	(SP)	151	29	(s) Ocean City
Twin Harbors	(SP)	370	49	(s) Westport
Westport City Park (summer only)	(MP)	130	0	in Westport
Chinook (summer only)	(CP)	100	(#)	in Chinook
Fort Canby	(SP)	60	(#)	(sw) Ilwaco

*Offers free hot water in wash rooms in addition to coin-operated showers. Not recommended for tents in winter.

Total Number of Public Owned Campsites: 1,312

PRIVATELY OWNED:

Near main highway or on side roads within approx. 10 miles. Some privately owned sites are restricted to "adults only," "self-contained trailers only," etc. Most are open all year. Conditions vary from "primitive" to "comfortable." As private campgrounds frequently change ownership with resulting change of name, these facilities are listed by area and approximate numbers of grounds in each area.

Neah Bay to Forks	5 operators
La Push area	4 operators
Quinault area	1 operator
Pacific Beach to Brown Point ("Olympia Beaches" area)	8 operators
Point Chehalis to Cape Shoalwater ("Twin Harbors" area)	8 operators
Raymond area	1 operator
Bay Center area	2 operators
Long Beach Peninsula	18 operators
Chinook - Ilwaco area	5 operators

Approx. Number of Private Campsites: 1,000

PHOTO ABOVE: Pacific Beach, Washington, with State Park. Trailer/camper parking area immediately north of creek. "Dual-use" beach with glass floats on winter high tides and superior clamming on the low tides.

Private campground near Smith River, Calif., just south of the Oregon border.

Winter camping at Bullards Beach State Park near Bandon, Oregon. Camp Ranger collects fees "very early in the a.m." at each campsite.

OREGON

NAME OF PARK	TYPE	No. TENT SPACES	No. RV SPACES	NEAREST TOWN
Fort Stevens	(SP)(R)(W)	380	223	(sw) Hammond
Saddle Mountain	(SP)	9	0	(se) Seaside
Oswald West (hike ¼ mile with wheelbarrow)	(SP)	36	0	(s) Cannon Beach
Nehalem Bay	(SP)(R)	292	(#)	Nehalem/Manzanita
Barview	(CP)	125	39	(w) Garibaldi
Kilchis	(SF)	30	(#)	(n) Tillamook
Sand Beach	(FS)	20	5	(n) Pacific City
Cape Lookout	(SP)(R)(W)	193	53	(sw) Tillamook
Whalen Island	(CP)	40	(#)	(n) Pacific City
Cape Kiwanda	(CP)	20	0	(n) Pacific City
Neskowin	(FS)	12	0	(s) Neskowin
Devils Lake	(SP)(R)	68	32	in Lincoln City (2 areas)
North Creek	(FS)	16	2	(e) Kernville (2 areas)
Schooner Creek	(FS) (See: North Creek)			
Beverly Beach	(SP)(R)(W)	151	127	(n) Newport
South Beach	(SP)(R)	262	(#)	(s) Newport
Beachside	(SP)(R)	60	20	(s) Waldport
Tillicum Beach	(FS)	7	40	(s) Waldport
Cape Perpetua	(FS)	42	(#)	(s) Yachats
Rock Creek	(FS)	7	9	(s) Yachats
Washburne	(SP)	2	58	(n) Florence
Sutton Lake	(FS)	12	101	(n) Florence

Private trailer park at Harbor, Oregon, near mouth of Chetco River.

NAME OF PARK	TYPE	No. TENT SPACES	No. RV SPACES	NEAREST TOWN
Siuslaw Hbr Vista	(CP)	20	18	(nw) Florence
Honeyman	(SP)(R)(W)	316	66	(s) Florence
Carter Lake	(FS)	12	32	(s) Florence
Tahkenitch	(FS)	8	36	(n) Reedport
Windy Cove	(CP)	20	50	on Winchester Bay
Umpqua Lighthouse	(SP)	41	22	(s) Winchester Bay
Tugman	(SP)	115	(#)	(s) Reedsport
Eel Creek	(FS)	10	88	(n) North Bend
Bluebell Lake	(FS)	19	(#)	(nw) North Bend (2 areas)
Bastendorf Beach	(CP)	35	30	(s) Coos Bay
Sunset Bay	(SP)(R)	108	29	(sw) Coos Bay
Bullards Beach	(SP)(R)(W)	64	128	(n) Bandon
Cape Blanco	(SP)	58	(#)	(nw) Port Orford
Humbug Mountain	(SP)	71	30	(s) Port Orford
Harris Beach	(SP)(R)(W)	117	34	(n) Brookings
Loeb	(SP)	53	(#)	(ne) Brookings
Little Redwood	(FS)	11	(#)	(ne) Brookings
Winchuck	(FS)	8	(#)	(se) Brookings

Total Number of Public Owned Campsites: 4,186

PRIVATELY OWNED

(See remarks under Washington State private grounds.)

Columbia River to Otis	17 operators
South of Otis to Florence	24 operators
South of Florence to Bandon	9 operators
South of Bandon to California	8 operators

Approx. Number of Private Campsites: 1,300

Sources: Correspondence and maps, Washington State Parks Department, Olympia, spring 1977; Oregon State Parks Department, Salem, spring 1977; *National Park Service Camping Directory*, 1976; *Rand-McNally Guide to Campsites*, 1975; correspondence and lists, U.S. Forest Service Region 6, Portland, 1976. □

APPENDIX C

BICYCLING ALONG THE OREGON COAST

Oregon is the first state to enact a law specifying that a specific percentage of highway funds must be used for the construction of Walkways and Bicycle ways. Since the law went into effect, hundreds of miles of "bike paths" as they are usually called, have been built both in urban and country areas. Many of these paths are utilitarian and will be found in areas near schools. As time and funds permit, additional paths are being built. In some areas, engineers located bike paths on abandoned railroad right-of-ways. Bike paths have also been built near parks and along rivers and creeks where motor vehicles have no access.

In some instances where it has not been possible to build a path parallel to a highway, the roads have been widened to create official "bicycle lanes." Or, the width of the road has been reduced and a lane reserved for bicycles.

Along the Oregon Coast bicycle paths have been created on the sides of highways or have been specially built so bikers can now traverse the state from border-to-border staying on bike paths all the way.

Before setting out to conquer the entire coast, determine potential weather conditions for the time of year. It might be well to travel south-to-north, or the other way around depending on circumstances for it's better to have a tailwind than a headwind. Speed can be dangerous on some long down grades especially if there is an intersection or sharp turn at the bottom—frequent. Along some few remaining older sections of highway with old style asphalt the surface tends to become very slick after a rain. On steep hills where the road is narrow and full of curves, and where bikes have to share the pavement with motor vehicles, there is particular risk. One such length is between the junction of U.S. 101—U.S. 26 south of Seaside, and Cannon Beach. During winter be wary of icy spots. It might be well to get off and push bikes over bridges because the steel grating on some bridges catches tires easily as well as always being slick in wet weather.

Most bicyclists have read that to "argue" with a motor vehicle over right-of-way can be *deadly* for the bike rider. Statistics show this to be true. A slogan some bike riders *live* by is, "Give way and live" when motorists threaten a bicyclist.

It would be well to review the official definitions as set forth by the Motor Vehicles Division of the Oregon Department of Transportation.

**Bicycle Lane near Neskowin,
North Oregon Coast.**

In Oregon:

"Bicycle" means every device propelled by human power upon which any person may ride, having two tandem wheels either of which is more than fourteen inches in diameter, or having three wheels, all of which are more than fourteen inches in diameter.

"Public way" means any public highway, street, road, footpath or bicycle trail.

"Bicycle lane" means that part of the highway, adjacent to the roadway, designated by official signs or markings for use by persons riding bicycles.

"Bicycle trail" means a publicly owned and maintained lane or way designated for use as a bicycle route and includes both a bicycle lane and a bicycle path.

"Bicycle path" means a public way maintained for exclusive use by persons riding bicycles and designated as such by official signs and markings.

Effective July 1, 1976, Oregon traffic rules were changed by a law passed during the 1975 Legislature. In summary, these are the rules plus comments on matters frequently misunderstood.

EQUIPMENT

LIGHTS:

A bicycle or its rider must have a white light visible from a distance of at least 500 feet *in front* of the bicycle. The law also requires a red reflector or lighting device or material, big enough and so mounted that it can be seen from all distances up to 600 feet *to the rear* when directly in front of motor vehicles headlights on low beam. These lighting requirements apply when a bicycle is being ridden on a highway from a half-hour after sunset to a half-hour before sunrise; or at any other time when people or vehicles cannot be clearly seen 500 feet ahead because of light or weather conditions.

Reflectors bolted onto spokes of wheels or onto peddles make attractive additions to bicycles. These reflectors may be used but must be in addition to the front light and rear red light or red reflector as prescribed. Amber reflector on rear of a bicycle is not acceptable in lieu of red. A white tail light is not acceptable on any vehicle—motor or bike in Oregon.

161

BRAKES:

Every bicycle must be equipped with a brake that permits the bicyclist to make the brake wheels skid on dry, level, clean pavement.

AUDIBLE SIGNAL DEVICES:

It is *against the law* to install or use a siren or whistle on a bicycle. Note that the regulation includes the word, "install" as well as the "use" of sirens or whistles. Horns, either electric or CO_2 cartridge operated may be used.

Take a
CLOSER
LOOK
Operating an unlawfully equipped bicycle is a Class D traffic infraction and could result in a fine of up to fifty dollars. A parent or guardian of any child or ward may be cited for allowing or knowingly permitting a child or ward to ride a bicycle that is not legally equipped.

RIDING RULES:

Every person riding a bicycle on a road is required to obey all traffic laws that apply to the driver of a motor vehicle, except those which by their nature cannot apply to a bicycle.

One must ride on or astride a permanent and regular seat attached to the bicycle. A bicycle must not be used to carry more persons at a time than the number for which it is designed and equipped.

Do not carry any package, bundle or article that prevents keeping at least one hand on the handlebar and having full control at all times. Do not "hitch" a ride by attaching the rider or the bicycle to a motor vehicle.

Do not ride more than two abreast. Bicycle riders must exercise due care when passing a standing vehicle or one going in the same direction. Ride as near to the right side of the road or street as practicable. On a one-way street *in a city,* bicyclists may ride as near as practicable to either the right of left side of the road.

If a bicycle lane or bicycle path is adjacent to a road, bicycle riders must use the lane or path, not the regular street or road, as long as the path or lane has been determined safe for bicycle use at reasonable rates of speed.

Bike racing is prohibited on bicycle lanes and paths. Littering bike right-of-ways is covered in the general regulations concerning littering on public roads.

BICYCLES AND MOTOR VEHICLES:

Drivers of motorized vehicles are not allowed to use a bicycle lane except when making a turn, entering or leaving an alley, private road or driveway, or when required during official duty, such as delivering the mail. Right-of-way must be yielded to bicycles using the bicycle lane.

Drivers of vehicles are not allowed to drive or park on a bicycle path.

WHO HAS THE RIGHT - OF - WAY ?

At intersections where traffic is regulated by signs or signals, bicyclists and drivers of other vehicles must stop or yield if they are facing a sign or signal that requires this action.

At intersections which are *not* controlled by signs or signals, bicycle riders are required to yield right of way to all vehicles within or closely approaching the intersection. There are two exceptions: A bicycle rider does not have to yield if the closely approaching vehicles from the opposite direction are signaling an intent or starting to make a left turn at the intersection, or if the approaching vehicles are required to stop for a stop sign before entering the intersection. (Extra care is required in intersections, especially those with heavy traffic. Never try to defend your right-of-way when on a bike. On a bicycle you will lose.)

■ *Drivers of motor vehicles making left turns or stopping at a stop sign who*
■ *fail to yield to bike riders in or close enough to an intersection to create*
■ *an immediate hazard may be cited for a Class B traffic infraction.*

A bicyclist who has been forced to take evasive action because of a motorist's failure to give legal right-of-way to a bicycle, has the right to make a citizens arrest of the motorist. Generally, a bike rider cannot catch a motor vehicle, but the rider should take down the license number, note the exact location and time of day. With these data any law enforcement officer can investigate the situation and have the bicyclist sign a complaint. If a bike is damaged by a motor vehicle (no personal injury) and the motorist leaves, this is hit-and-run Class A infraction. If the bicyclist is injured and the motorist leaves the scene, the motorist may be charged with a Class C Felony crime.

Under Oregon law a bike cannot be ridden on a sidewalk in a commercial (business) zone, but under some conditions, bicycles can be ridden on sidewalks in residential zones. The major points regarding bikes and walkers are 1. An audible warning before overtaking and passing a pedestrian on a sidewalk must be given. 2. Pedestrians have the right-of-way on sidewalks. Careless operation of a bike on a sidewalk so as to endanger *"or would be likely to endanger any person or property"* (ORS 487:43:785) might be classed as reckless driving—including such acts on private property.

"Speeding" on bicycles may bring arrest as with a motor vehicle. Likewise, "weaving" in and out of traffic may be the cause for citation. In some areas, bike paths cross and usually signs as seen on highways are used to caution bicyclists—the signs are miniature size. There have been collisions of bikes and injuries to riders and walkers at bike path crossings when a cyclist has failed to heed posted signs, particularly STOP signs. Citations and complaints may be issued for traffic violations between bicycles, and between bicycles and pedestrians.

★　　★　　★　　★

Sources: The Oregon law that authorized bicycle paths, plus additional laws that govern the use of bicycles and the paths are covered in the *Oregon Revised Statutes (ORS). ORS 366, 383, 486, 487.* The 1975 changes are incorporated into statutes cited.

★　　★　　★　　★

A summary for bicycle riders appears in pamphlet form available from Oregon Department of Motor Vehicle offices. *See: Oregon's NEW Bicycle Rules of the Road.* Motor Vehicles Division, Dept. of Transportation (Salem), 1976. □

APPENDIX D

IDENTIFYING DRIFTWOOD

Along the Northwest Coast there are few restrictions on picking up miscellaneous pieces of driftwood of any size. In some areas, saws are permitted and on certain beaches a truck can be taken for driftwood salvage for personal use. It is true, that some who live along the coast pick driftwood on a continuing basis solely for heating their homes. Probably the most common use for driftwood is for home fireplaces.

Driftwood comes in uncountable numbers of forms. Some resembles animals or manmade objects and these pieces are often kept to display and to talk about.

The number of lumber mills near the ocean in the states of the Pacific Northwest is quite large and many of these operations are often near rivers. Fresh logs sometimes break away from log rafts and are lost to the rivers. Heavy rains of the region wash out riverbank trees, thus these logs and trees float downstream, enter the ocean, and are eventually distributed along the coast on incoming tides. Accordingly, the Northwest Coast is probably the best area of all the United States mainland for driftwood seekers.

Seldom does one pick up a piece of driftwood without thinking or asking questions, "What kind of wood is this?" "Where did this come from?"

Recalling the chapter (7) on ocean currents, one can see that varieties of wood common to California can be carried to Northwest Coast beaches on the Davidson

Current. Redwood, a native of Northern California and in Southwest Oregon, can be found on Washington and Alaska beaches. As has been seen, coves collect driftwood during winter storms.

Through the Oregon State University Extension Service, Sea Grant Marine Advisory Program, dozens of woods, common along the Oregon coast, have been identified and their frequency of occurrence is such that driftwood fanciers will want to know more about them.

Identifying driftwood is a science. It depends upon how exacting one wishes to be as to how scientific he will be about it.

Of more than eighty types of trees commercially logged in the U.S., over two dozen of these can probably be found as driftwood along the Northwest Coast. In addition, do not forget that the ocean currents will deposit logs and lumber lost from ships at sea along the beaches. Often these are exotic types.

One needs realize that some positive identifications can only be made with a microscope. But our purpose here is to present an overview of driftwood identification. It is necessary to know that some oriental woods have similar characteristics to native woods. Also, woods that have been soaking in the ocean for long periods of time may have their anatomical features altered. Driftwood identification can be a real challenge. For the investigative beachcomber, it opens new fields for exploration.

A magnifying glass is needed since wood is made up of great numbers of cells. Each wood has its own cell characteristics. By studying these cells, along with observing color, texture, weight, degrees of softness or hardness—and the aroma—the wood can be identified. The more practice one has with wood identification, the more fascinating the experience becomes.

HAND TOOLS FOR IDENTIFYING DRIFTWOOD

It is often easy to tell the *gross* differences of woods with the naked eye. However, for more positive (*anatomical*) identification, a magnifying lens, a sharp pocket knife and a saw are required.

Probably the easiest kind of a lens to carry is a hand lens tied to a string and worn around the neck. A 6X lens is minimal. A 10X lens is better. Some hand lenses have a swivel with two glasses to allow viewing through either lens. One looks through both lenses for even greater magnification. Jeweler's loops—the lens watchmakers seem to hold in an eye while working, can also be used but such loops are cumbersome to carry. Persons who normally wear glasses and who

Swiss Army Knife and 10X lens.

are continually doing closeup work can have a small, extreme closeup lens cemented on the corner of their glasses.

The knife needs to have a blade about three inches long and be very sharp. Large hunting knives or razor blades can be used but these can be dangerous. A small hand saw is generally permissible on beaches where commercial chain saws are sometimes questioned. If a saw is to be used, care should be taken to minimize damage to the teeth caused by nails, sand, and imbedded shells.

ABOUT SAWS: For salvaging a section of log to take home for later study, a bow saw is probably the easiest to carry and to use. Although available in a variety of sizes, there is little reason to burden one's self by packing a saw with greater than a nineteen inch blade. Bow saws have about four teeth to the inch. These teeth will tear into almost anything. Children should not play with a bow saw. Bow saws are excellent for use on firewood.

The most common household saw is the "crosscut." This saw can be used with excellent results for clean cutting across a log. A saw that is sharp and has a good "set" gives the best cut. For very fine cross cutting, a cabinet maker's "finish" saw might be used. A finishing saw is a crosscut but shorter in length and with smaller teeth closer together. A "rip" saw is for cutting *with the grain* of a log or board. While a crosscut saw can be used to "rip" a piece of wood, the sawing is tedious. To use a rip saw to cut the end off a log, (across the grain), will yield a very jagged cut. All saws, regardless of type or size should have a protector on the blade when being carried. A protector can be made with a folded double thickness of cardboard taped around the blade.

There are three major *surfaces* of wood to be aware of.

1. CROSS SECTION - as when a log is sawn in two and one looks at the butt. The annual rings are easily visible.
2. RADIAL SURFACE - as when a log is sawn lengthwise. A radial cut requires a "ripsaw" as opposed to the common "crosscut" saw.
3. TANGENTIAL SURFACE - is that part of the log first seen after peeling off the bark.

✱　　✱　　✱　　✱

SOME WORDS ESSENTIAL TO THE UNDERSTANDING OF WOOD

ANNUAL GROWTH RINGS - form each spring in trees growing in temperate climatic zones. When the tree is dormant in winter, growth stops. When growing starts the following year, a new ring develops.

AROMA (odor) - may be used as an identifier on freshly cut logs but on wood that has been in the sea, or in the sun bleaching on a beach for a considerable time may be odorless. With the bow saw, cut off the end of the log, or make a cut into the wood to reach the heartwood. The driftwood investigator can place his nose close to the "kerf" (the slot cut by the saw) and sniff. (As in all sniff tests, one should partially fill the lungs with fresh air before sniffing any sample.) Odors of woods can sometimes be enhanced by moistening the freshly cut area with a rag that was dampened in fresh (not salt) water. Woods are generally known for their fresh, outdoorsy smells. If an odor from a piece of driftwood is decidedly unpleasant, it may be caused by molds or fungi.

COLOR - generally applied to heartwood. Oregon myrtlewood, walnut, and redwood contain distinctive colors. Color alone will not identify a wood. In driftwood, color often changes because of salt water.

GRAIN AND TEXTURE - terms applied to figure, or pattern of wood as seen on radial and tangential surfaces by the growth rings, and by studying of cells and colorations. Grain and texture are often described as even or uneven; interlocked; vertical; flat; or straight.

HARDNESS - can only be technically evaluated in a laboratory. However relative hardness can be determined by pressing a thumbnail or the edge of a knife against the grain.

HARDWOODS - the deciduous trees (shed leaves in fall). But there are exceptions which the driftwood specialist will want to investigate.

HEARTWOOD - the inner growth. In many trees the heartwood is darker in color. For some woods, as red alder and true firs, there is almost no color difference.

LATEWOOD (summerwood) - is darker than springwood, forms late in the season. It is darker and more dense.

SAPWOOD - the new growth on the outside circumference of a log but not including the bark.

SOFTWOOD - also called evergreens and conifers.

SPRINGWOOD (early wood) - the part of an annual ring that develops at the start of the growing season. Early wood can be detected because it is light colored.

WEIGHT - of a wood will assist with identification. Weight varies depending on whether the wood is wet or dry.

HARDWOODS AND SOFTWOODS ON OREGON BEACHES

Identifying Characteristics of woods marked * are in this book.

HARDWOODS	SOFTWOODS
American Elm	Alaska-cedar (Alaska Yellow-cedar)
American (West Indies) Mahogany	Douglas-fir (old growth)*
Beech	Douglas-fir (young growth)
Birch	Incense-cedar
Black Cherry	Lodgepole Pine
Black Cottonwood	Pacific Yew
Black Walnut	Ponderosa Pine
California Black Oak	Port Orford-cedar*
Hickories	Redwood*
Lauans (Philippine Mahogany)	Sitka Spruce*
Oregon Ash	Southern Pine(s)
Oregon Maple (Bigleaf Maple)	Sugar Pine
Oregon-myrtle (California laurel) *	True Firs
Oregon White Oak	Western Hemlock
Pacific Dogwood	Western Juniper
Pacific Madrone*	Western Larch
Red Alder*	Western Red cedar
Redgum (Sweetgum)	Western White Pine*
And others	And others

MAGNIFYING GLASS SCRUTINY ON CROSSCUTS:

POROUS AND NONPOROUS. A major difference between hardwood and softwood is that hardwood has pores (vessels) in the rings. Softwoods do not have pores.

TRACHEIDS AND RESIN CANALS. With a glass, one can easily see resin canals in tracheids (cells) of Douglas fir, pines, spruce and western larch. Tracheids are cells in softwoods arranged in radial rows across growth rings. The resin canals appear as large round openings. In woods other than listed, these cells seem as white specks.

WOOD RAYS. These ribbonlike masses of cells extending from the bark toward the center of a log, when examined on a cross cut, appear as lines, in varying widths, running generally at right angles to annual rings. In softwoods, rays are nearly indistinguishable. Rays in hardwood are more easily seen as narrow lines. In oak, wood rays can be seen by sharp-eyed without a glass.

✷   ✷   ✷   ✷

TYPICAL OREGON DRIFTWOOD

DOUGLAS-FIR (old growth)
Pseudotsuga menzieü
(State Tree of Oregon)

Next to Redwoods, Douglas-fir is the largest tree of the Pacific Coast, Rocky Mountains, Canada, Mexico. Microscope necessary for positive identity because of resemblance with Western Larch in some characteristics. A softwood without pores and sparse resin canals. Abrupt change in cellular construction across growth ring. Sparse resin canals appear as pairs. Distinct, narrow growth rings may be wavy looking—a slow-to-grow tree. Sapwood pale yellow to off-white. Heartwood yellow to light red-brown. Abrupt change between early and late wood. Summerwood is dark. *Principal timber tree in U.S. in stand, dimension lumber, veneer.* Used in laminated arches, fences, furniture, floors, boats, ladders. Common firewood.

OREGON-MYRTLE (California-laurel)
Umbellularia calfornica

Moderately hardwood and quite heavy. Pores barely visible with magnifying glass. Classed as "diffuse porus" since pores are very uniform. Very narrow wood rays visible to naked eye. Distinct growth rings separated by dark tissue. Sapwood is cream color with variations to brown. Wide color range in heartwood from tan through reddish-brown to brown. Very spicy aroma. Myrtlewood is an outstanding specie for machine turning. Its surface polishes to mirrorlike brilliance. Ideal for furniture, especially table tops, gunstocks, trays, dishes, bowls. "Myrtlewood factories" along the Oregon Coast Highway, particularly in the North Bend-Coos Bay area, have extensive showrooms and often offer guided tours of their plants.

NOTE: Contrary to statements of operators of many "myrtlewood factories" and gift shops, myrtlewood *trees* have no relationship to the myrtlewood *bush* of biblical reference. Myrtlewood trees, commonly known as California-laurel, grow abundantly along the coast from about Coos Bay, Oregon, to south of Los Angeles, California, as well as through inland Northern California east of the Sacramento and Northern San Joaquin Valleys. The inland belt skirts the west side of Lake Tahoe and dwindles near Yosemite National Park. Many of these trees have multiple trunks and symmetrical shape. Although broadleafed, myrtlewood trees do not shed leaves in winter.

PACIFIC MADRONE
Arbutus menziesii

Very heavy reddish-brown hardwood. Pores diffuse class, numerous and uniform of size except one row of larger pores appear at start of each annual ring, all barely visible under glass. Note band of tissue alternating with zones of pores. Very fine rays quite narrow and barely visible with glass. Extreme hardness makes madrone difficult to saw, but easy for lathe turning. Used in furniture, plywood, toys, ideal for long rollers up to eight-inches diameter for moving cargoes on

Freshly cut Oregon Myrtle (California-laurel).

ships. Two-inch madrone ideal for moving pianos across residential floors. Long burning wood for fireplaces.

PORT ORFORD-CEDAR
Chamaecyparis lawsoniana

Medium textured softwood without pores or resin canals. Heartwood with either fragrant, spicy, pungent, sometimes raw potato aroma. Yellowish or light brown coloring but may become darker after being in seawater. Pale color of sapwood might not be defined from heartwood. Annual rings inconspicuous. A "heavy" wood, suitable for tooling, turning. Used for arrow shafts, canoe paddles, boats, "cedar chests," mothproofing closets, musical instruments, furniture, cabinet work and artifacts.

RED ALDER
Alnus rubra

Moderately soft and light weight, with diffuse pores. Two sizes of rays: Quite narrow and hard to see with glass. Other larger, randomly spaced and in crosscut may be seen with naked eye.

Indistinct separation between sapwood and heartwood. Fresh cut logs usually warm (cream) white but turns toward reddish or light brown after cut. Annual rings very clear. Carves and works easily. Noted for smooth surface. Commonly used in furniture, toys, pulp.

REDWOOD
Sequoia sempervirens
Coarse textured softwood without pores or resin canals. No general smell however heartwood sometimes has unpleasant odor. Distinct reddish-brown heartwood but some examples may run to light tan. Cellular changes are abrupt from spring to summer. Redwood is very light weight and easy to cut for firewood, however can be difficult to cut for artifacts unless care is taken by using small-tooth (finishing) saw because the wood is *very* soft. Redwood, an extremely durable wood, was used in mid-1930's in Golden Gate Bridge, San Francisco, since redwood withstands weathering. Noted for use in coffins, shingles, vats, tanks, outdoor furniture, fences, plywood, novelties. A burl from a redwood log as a home decoration will usually sprout and start a new tree. Do not confuse redwood with incense-cedar and Western cedar. Redwood lacks the cedar smell.

SITKA SPRUCE
Picea sitchenis
Softwood for which there was great demand in the First World War years for light-weight "aeroplane" spars. No pores. Has sparse resin canals with cell sizes changing gradually across growth ring. Sapwood varies from pale brown to pink-tinted yellows. Sometimes lavender cast. Heartwood ranges from pinkish yellows to light brown. After exposure, color may darken to silver-brown with trace of red. Distinct annual rings with uniform texture. Spring-and summer-wood blends at meeting point. Few resin canals. Minimal aroma. Used for boxes and crates, floor, laminated beams, general building lumber.

WESTERN WHITE PINE
Pinus monticola
Very soft, light, uniform texture without pores but with numerous resin canals with cell sizes changing across growth ring. The small cells and canals generally identifiable without a glass. Narrow to medium wide sapwood is pale yellow to off-white. Heartwood is more cream-colored running light and/or reddish-brown. Annual rings very uniform and distinct however little distinction between early and latewood. Glass needed to see resin canals. Wood has resin aroma when freshly cut. All of the pines are used as "knotty pine" paneling; general construction. Easy to work by hand or machine. Piano keys, matchsticks, picture frames, organ pipes, plywood.

★　　★　　★　　★

Sources: For this book, eight trees whose woods are commonly found as driftwood are used to orient driftwood enthusiasts to the techniques of wood identification. Naturally, there are many more woods of which thirty-four are identified in: Van Vliet, pp. 2-3, 5-10, 16, 26-27, 28, 32-34, 40-41. No method of "eyeballing" a stick of driftwood and identifying it has been discovered.

For a discussion about "Oregon Myrtlewood" trees (California-laurel) [*Umbellularia california*] see: *Trees: The Yearbook of Agriculture 1949*. U.S. Dept. of Agriculture, U.S. Gov. Print Office, 1949, pp. 809-810.

Ross, Charles R. *Trees to Know in Oregon*. [Extension Bulletin 697] Oregon State Univ. Extension Service/Oregon State Forestry Dept. Rev. Ed. 1975. pp. 64-65. □

APPENDIX E

STARFISH PRESERVATION

Make a 4 per cent solution of formalin by diluting commercial formaldehyde 9:1 (nine parts of water to one part of formaldehyde). The quantity to be made depends upon the number of starfish to be preserved and the size of container used. The solution should be deep enough to at least cover the starfish when they are placed in it. The starfish should be in the shape desired when placed in the formalin.

Shaping can usually be accomplished by placing the animals in a container of salt water just prior to preserving and letting them move about on their own accord. After placing the stars in formalin, they should be left standing for 2 to 3 days, then removed, rinsed off with fresh water, and allowed to dry at room temperature or in the sun. With this method there is a slight odor of formalin for a few days, but this will disappear in a short time. If properly done, there will be no odor of decaying fish.

★　　★　　★　　★

Sources: Walter G. Schroeder, Oregon State University Extension Agent for Curry County, Oregon, provided the data on starfish preservation which had been prepared earlier by Oregon Dept. of Fish and Wildlife. □

South jetty, Coquille River (Bandon) on a very disturbed January day. (*See*: pages 120-121.)

APPENDIX F

RAINY DAYS AND WHAT TO DO WITH THEM

For most, there is surely nothing exciting about being forced to stay in a tent or camper because it rains. Many a week's vacation has been "ruined because it rained," but these "ruinations" probably came about due to lack of forethought.

All who live along the Northwest Coast know that it rains there, and sooner or later those who visit the area will find it out. As has been mentioned in this book, the weather along the coast of Washington and Oregon is varied. Beachcombing activities do not come to a halt because of weather or low/high tide. However, what one forages for and how one goes about it will vary depending on the weather and tides. Because the calendar says it is summer, and because most vacations come in summer does not guarantee "summer" (hot) weather.

Visitors to the Northwest Coast will want to plan for both hot, sunny days as well as for those which are clammy and wet. (The best beachcombing for glass floats is on wet, winter, stormy days. This has been discussed.) In Chapter 3, there is mention that drippy weather is nearly normal for July and August in the north Washington area. In Chapter 4, the writers tell about the cool (foggy?) south Oregon coast while people in the inland (Willamette and Rogue) valleys swelter.

One summer, the authors spent a couple of weeks in Southeast Idaho. When it was time to return to Oregon, we took regular shifts at driving in order to get out of the desert, across the mountains and to the cool coast. When we got to Salem (via McKenzie Pass), we stopped only long enough for gas and to again soak our heads before pushing on into the cool, glorious, *f—o—g* which met us (on that day) near Lincoln City. (Possibly many inland residents go to the beach to cool off and not for beachcombing—we had not thought of that before!)

Once in early August, a research trip was being made to Tillamook Rock aboard the Coast Guard Buoy-tender *Tupelo*. The day started sunny and just right. We crossed the Columbia River bar and the "chop" became choppier. Fog closed in. The skipper approached the Rock but we could not find it except on radar. No pictures that day. We were back at Tongue Point by afternoon and saw that the weather had turned cool and gray there too. Our trip was not lost because we had winter coats, wool socks and hiking boots along. We stayed on the coast all that week and found much to do other than sit and mope about the weather. Sure enough—on the way home the sun came out!

And so it is. Toss a coin and guess the weather on the Northwest Coast. Because it is raining in Portland it does not mean it is raining in Astoria—or the other way around. Radio and television weather forecasts can be depended upon to a degree. But the best backup system for not allowing the weather to "washout" a vacation is to carry clothing for both wet and dry conditions.

Too much rain is however, too much rain. There is a point where coast campers need something to do inside. There is only so much room in a tent or camper to hang wet things (which never seem to get dry), and only limited corners in which to stash them.

Every coastal visitor should have a backup plan especially if children are along and the rain becomes overbearing. Games of all sorts that are compact and have a minimal of number of little parts that can get lost easily are essential. Consider these: Cards. Checkers or chess. Dominoes. Book of hand tricks. Tape recorder and have a "funny-noise" contest. Book of jokes. Cross-word puzzles. Scrabble (have a dictionary). Knitting. Drawing. Coloring. Read-alouds where everyone reads from the same book—but make certain the story is interesting! Bring the kids up for air and let them run in the rain for a few minutes when the closeness of a tent brings on frayed edges. Better, *parents run with them* for steam needs venting by adults too. The "Beachcombers Boiled Bucket Banquet" (*See:* Appendix A, No. 11) can be started and the family-run-for-fresh-air might occur while the banquet boils.

Those with trailers or other types of RV's are not glued to the site as tenters might be. But tenters can take off too. Button up (take small valuables along), tell the camp manager when you expect to be back, and head for the nearest town's museum and library. Or, see about visiting a Coast Guard lighthouse if you are reasonably close to one.

Museums are many, and some are small and operate on irregular hours. There is generally a museum in each County Seat. Locate these on your road map. The "Visitor's Bureau" in Chamber of Commerce offices list the local museums and libraries. Also see the Yellow Pages in the phone books under "Museums." Some museums, operated by historical societies, have no phones but local people will know where they are.

An excellent way to spend a rainy day is at Fort Columbia in the maritime museum. Kids love museums if the stay is not too long. If parents are equipped with a book telling of coastal history, both the museum visit and the book become more fun.

Astoria not only has the Clatsop County Historical Society Museum, but the Columbia River Maritime Museum along side of which is docked the retired Coast Guard lightship *Columbia* (fee). During posted hours, visitors can go abroad the Coast Guard cutters at Tongue Point, east of Astoria, as well as the ocean-going Coast Guard (armed) tug docked near the old lightship. If there is no sign posted at ship's dock, go aboard and ask if a tour can be arranged. Other noted museums are in Tillamook (Pioneer Museum); Lincoln City and Newport. The Marine Science Center, Oregon State University, is at Newport. There is a U.S. Forest Service Interpretive Exhibit at Cape Perpetua south of Yachats (YAH-HOTS). Sea Lion Caves was mentioned earlier in the book (fee). There are thrills on the Dune Buggy rides (fee), between Florence and North Bend, rain or shine. The museum at the end of the bridge on the Coast Highway in North Bend is open long hours. An excellent museum is operated by the Curry County Historical Society at Gold Beach. The Chetco Valley Museum is just south of Brookings. Most of the major museums have book sales counters.

At this writing, display materials about the bombing of the mainland of the United States by an Imperial Japanese Navy plane are in the Chetco Valley Museum. Bomb fragments are in the U.S. Forest Service Chetco Ranger Station in Brookings. In the Brookings Police station, in a Myrtlewood display case, is the Samurai-type sword presented to the people of Brookings by former Imperial pilot, Nobuo Fujita, when he visited the city in 1962. He and his son gave the family sword in apology for the aerial bombing of the continental United States in 1942.

In Crescent City are several museums, the most picturesque being on Battery

Clatsop Plains Presbyterian Church is oldest continuing Presbyterian Church west of Rockies, founded Sept. 19, 1846. Communion Table is of cedar driftwood from nearby beach.

Point. Access is by walking during low tide (dry ground) to the former Coast Guard lighthouse. The Battery Point museum has parts from the *S.S. Emidio* which was attacked by Japanese submarine *I-17* early in the war. Although reported by the Japanese as "sunk," *Emidio* drifted onto a rock near Battery Point where it remained until 1959 when it was dismantled as a hazard to navigation.

Policy changes make it impossible to list those public libraries which loan books to campers who are registered in nearby State Parks. Some do. Ask at the desk. Many libraries are branches which operate on local schedules.

PUBLIC LIBRARIES ALONG THE NORTHWEST COAST

Scott's No. 1584.
Dec. 8, 1977

WASHINGTON	OREGON	
Aberdeen	Astoria	North Bend
Forks	Bandon	Port Orford
Hoquiam	Bay City	Reedsport
Ilwaco	Brookings	Seaside
North Beach	Cannon Beach	Tillamook
Ocean Park	Coos Bay	
Ocean Shores	Florence	
Pacific Beach	Garibaldi	CALIFORNIA
Port Angeles	Gold Beach	Crescent City
Raymond	Langlois	
South Bend	Lincoln City	
Taholah	Manzanita	
Westport	Newport	

Reading room and book stacks in Astoria Public Library, Astoria, Oregon.

GENERAL REFERENCES

California; a Guide to the Golden State. [American Guide Series] Federal Writer's Project. Hastings Rev. Ed. 1967.

Clark, Lewis J. *Wildflowers of the Sea Coast.* Gray. Sidney, B.C. 1974.

Cotter, Charles S. *The Physical Geography of the Oceans.* American Elsevier, 1966.

Light List, Pacific Coast and Pacific Islands, Vol. III. U.S. Coast Guard, 1972.

Oregon; End of the Trail. [American Guide Series] Federal Writer's Project. Binfords & Mort. 1940. Rev. Ed. 1951.

Nehls, Harry B. *Familiar Birds of Northwest Shores and Waters.* Portland Audubon Society. (Oregon)1975.

Shepard, Francis P. *Our Changing Coastlines.* McGraw-Hill, 1971.

Smith, Lynwood S. *Living Shores of the Pacific Northwest.* Pacific Search Press. 1976.

Sverdrup, H.D., Martin, W. Johnson, and Richard H. Fleming. *The Oceans.* Prentice-Hall, 1942. (cited as Sverdrup)

Thompson, Bob. (Ed.) *Beachcomber's Guide to the Pacific Coast.* Lane. 1968.

The United States Coast Survey 35th Congress 2nd Session. Executive Document No. 14. 1859.

U.S. Coast Pilot 7, Pacific Coast, 8th edition. U.S. Coast and Geodetic Survey, 1959.

Van Vliet, Antone C. and Alexis J. Panshin. *Identifying Oregon Driftwood.* Oregon State Univ. Extension Service/Sea Grant Advisory Program. [Extension Manual 2] 1976. ($1.25 postpaid from Oregon State Univ. Extension Service. Oregon State Univ. Corvallis, Oregon 97331.)

Waaland, J. Robert. *Common Seaweeds of the Pacific Coast.* Pacific Search Press. 1977.

Washington; A Guide to the Evergreen State. [American Guide Series] Federal Writer's Project. Binfords & Mort. 1941. Rev. Ed. 1950.

Webber, Bert. *Beachcombing for Driftwood, for Glass Floats, for Agates, for Fun.* Ye Galleon, Rev. Ed. 1973 (cited as Webber, *Beachcombing*)

_____. *The Hero of Battle Rock.* Ye Galleon. Expanded Ed. 1978.

_____. *RETALIATION: Japanese Attacks and Allied Countermeasures Along the Pacific Coast in World War II.* Oregon State Univ. Press, 1975. (cited as, Webber, *Retaliation:*)

_____. *What Happened at Bayocean—Is Salishan Next?* Ye Galleon, Expanded Ed. 1973.

Wood, Amos L. *Beachcombing for Japanese Glass Floats.* Binfords & Mort, 1967. Rev. Ed. 1971. (cited as Wood (Binford)

_____. *Beachcombing the Pacific.* Regnery. 1975. (cited as Wood (Regnery)

Zahl, Paul A. "Oregon's Sidewalk on the Sea," in *National Geographic Magazine.* November 1961. pp. 708-734.

About the closest the U.S. Postal Service has come to a stamp for beachcombing to date, is this set of four *se-tennant* 2¢ values for the National Parks Centennial showing Cape Hatteras National Seashore. Scott's Nos. 1448-49-50-51 issued April 5, 1972.

SOURCES

ACKNOWLEDGEMENTS

AND NOTES

NOTES FOR CHAPTER 1: (None)

NOTES FOR CHAPTER 2: (None)

NOTES FOR CHAPTER 3:
SOME FEATURES OF THE NORTHWEST COAST (OVERVIEW)

Armstrong, Chester H. *Oregon State Parks History 1917-1963*. Oregon State Highway Commission, 1965.

Light List, Pacific Coast and Pacific Islands, Vol. III, U.S. Coast Guard, 1972.

Monaghan, Robert. *Pronunciation Guide of Oregon Place Names*. Oregon Assn. of Broadcasters, 1961.

Oregon, End of the Trail. pp. 363-387.

U.S. Coast Pilot 7, Pacific Coast.
Washington [American Guide Series] pp. 554-556, 557-567.

Webber, *RETALIATION:* pp. 54, 58, 83-86.

_____, "Southern Oregon Coast Major Factor in Marketing Easter Today," in, *Oregon Journal,* April 7, 1971. Sec. 2. p. 1.

_____, "Got Any Fresh Fruits...California Border Inspection." in, *Oregon Journal,* July 12, 1972. Sec. 2. p. 1.

"Tribal Ordnance Title 52," Quinault Indian Nation (known as the Beach Lands Ordinance of the Quinault Indian Reservation), March 28, 1970, cites Presidential Executive Order of November 4, 1873, pursuant to Treaty of July 1, 1855, 12 Stat. 971, as "land includ[ing] beach lands along the Pacific Ocean above the 'low water mark'...no person shall deface or destroy natural beauty, objects of nature [or take from:] sand, rock, mineral, marine growth, *driftwood,* fish, wildlife, *agates,* or *souveniers or other products of the beach lands.* No fires, no tent or

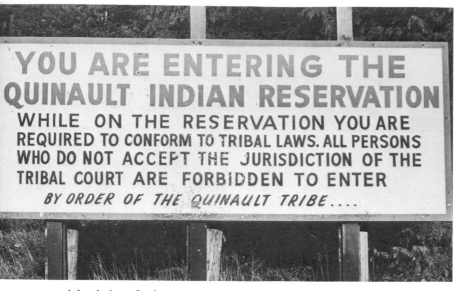

Sign on Highway 109 south of Taholah, Washington.

overnight shelter, [no] overnight camping...without permits issued by the Business Committee," Quinault Indian Nation, Taholah, Wash. 98587." *(Italics added.)*

Title 52.05 provides for "Physical ejection" from the Reservation and possible "prosecution in the Tribal Court" for trespass without a permit. Further, equipment of trespassers "May be confiscated."

A letter from Thomas E. Purkey, Land Use Planner, Quinault Indian Nation, Sept. 1976 includes: "Presently the Tribal Council issues very few beach use permits to persons who are not tribal members or employees. The beach closure is strictly enforced by the Tribal Trespass Patrol. Reservation beaches are *not* [italics his] open to beachcombing."

"Closure of Beaches" in *Nugguam* [Translation: Talk], Vol. 5. No. 12, Taholah, Wash., Sept. 5, 1969, states that on Aug. 25, 1969 the Quinault Indian Reservation beaches were closed to the public because real estate developers' heavy equipment removes sand—tribal property; improper disposal of sewage, "the public has been carrying away large amounts of driftwood," "...beauty of Point Grenville vandalized by paint and dumping of trash by campers...illegal clam digging, driftwood fires...." ☐

NOTES FOR CHAPTER 4:
A CLOSE LOOK AT THE OREGON COAST

At this writing Thomas Creek Safety Rest Area is undeveloped except for parking lot and view. Information on the *Marjean* will be found in *Pacific Powerland,* Pacific Power & Light Co., Portland, 1971 No. 1, p. 2. "Salishan Sailor Builds Sleek 46-Foot Sailboat—of Cement!"

Lincoln City *News Guard,* Jan. 4, 11, 1973. News stories with photos of beached *Marjean.*

Dicken, Samuel N. *Pioneer Trails of the Oregon Coast,* Oregon Historical Society. 1971.
Mr. Dicken's work is illustrated with maps then illuminated with current photographs many being aerials from offshore angles clearly showing the beaches.

Gibbs, James A. *Shipwrecks of the Pacific Coast.* Binford & Mort, 1962, pp. 162-163.

Miller, Emma Gene. *Clatsop County, Oregon.* Binford & Mort, 1958. p. 105.

Webber, *Bayocean—Salishan.*

—————, *Hero of Battle Rock.*

—————, *RETALIATION:* Mines at Columbia River, pp. 54, 65, 81. Beach Patrols, 79-89. ☐

NOTES FOR CHAPTER 5: (None)

NOTES FOR CHAPTER 6: *VELELLA*

Velella: Phylum Coelenterata. *CLASS 1. HYDROZOA.* Order 1. Hydroida. Suborder 4. Chondrophora (Physolphorida).

Barnes, Robert D. *Invertebrate Zoology.* Saunders, 1968. pp. 92-94.

Hedgpeth, Joel W. *Between Pacific Tides.* 4th Ed. Stanford Univ. Press, 1968. pp. 226-228.

Nickols, David, *et al. Oxford Book of Invertebrates.* Orford Univ. Press, 1971. p. 10.

Storer, Tracy I. and Robert L. Usinger. *General Zoology.* McGraw-Hill, 1965. pp. 334-336.

   Velella is often confused with Portuguese Man-of-war. The latter is considerably larger, stings, and can kill. *Velella* has stingers but apparently only uses them on its food. Portuguese Man-of-war is same phylum and class as *Velella* but is Order 4, Siphonophora, found especially in warm seas—a tropical fish. Both are frequently called "jellyfish" which they are not. (Storer, p. 335.) □

NOTES FOR CHAPTER 7:
GLASS BALLS AND OCEANOGRAPHY

Bascom, Willard. *Waves and Beaches: The Dynamics of the Ocean Surface.* (Anchor Div. Doubleday, 1964) p. 20, offers a scientific description of the components of beaches of the north Pacific coast. *See Also:* Ch. IX, "Beaches".

Cotter, pp. 264-268.

   The name Kuroshio (*Kuro Siwo*) has been identified as "undoubtedly derived from the deep blue color of its water" as early as 1856, wrote a member of Commodore Perry's Japan Expedition, quoted in Maury, M.F. *The Physical Geography of the Sea.* 8th Ed. (Harper) 1869 p. 193

McGraw-Hill Encyclopedia of Science and Technology, "Coriolis Acceleration and Force," Vol. 3, p.535; "Sea-level Fluctuations; Effects of Coriolis Acceleration," Vol.12, p.151; "Tidal Currents." Vol.13, p.654.

   In addition to letters from Marine Science Center, OSU, Newport, Oregon, spring 1977, portions of this chapter were reviewed by Donald E. Giles, Marine Educational Specialist at the Center, and by Oceanographers on the Oregon State University campus, Corvallis. Edward J. Condon, Extension Oceanographer, O.S.U., provided photographs of *R/V Acona;* the freshly washed up drift bottle; and loaned Drift Card No. 25062 for study. The *Acona* was sold several years ago and was last reported to be operating in Alaska waters.
Sverdrup, pp. 712-728. □

Author, lecturer Amos L. Wood (left) discusses large amber float brought to Netarts-Oceanside-Cape Meares Beachcombers Festival on street in Oceanside.

NOTES FOR CHAPTER 8:
SIZES AND TYPES OF GLASS FLOATS

Stuart Farnsworth of Portland, Oregon, has a collection of glass fishing floats all of which are in *color*. He acquired many from friends and some from penpals. He traded for others. His is the most comprehensive color float collection yet seen by the authors. Here is a sample of his gathering by color and size. Of course he has many more than space here permits listing.

Amber	2.5", 3.3", 10.8"
Dark amber (hand blown)	3.3"
Dark amber (3-piece mold)	3.2"
Bromine amber (3-piece mold)	3.3"
Cobalt blue	3.1"
Dark royal blue	10.8"
Blue (Mason jar-blue button)	4.9"
Olive	4.8", 10.8"
Purple (dark brown button)	3.1"
Royal purple	4.9"
(appears black without strong backlight)	
Suntinted purple	
Aqua (coke bottle)	4.9"
Burnt umber	5", 10.7"
Dark smokeblue	3.2"
Dark skyblue	4.8"
Kelly green	3.3"

Additional colors Farnsworth has seen but does not own:
Pink, suntint pink, gray, Mason jar blue (vivid), Vics Vapo-rub brilliant blue, wine red, bright orange, smoky brown, brilliant green, lavender, lemon-lime.

Wood (Binford), pp. 188, 190-192. □

NOTES FOR CHAPTER 9:
BEWARE OF PHONY FLOATS

Webber, Bert. "There's Gold, of Sorts, in Pacific Flotsam and Jetsam," in *Oregon Journal*, February 23, 1971. Sec. 2, p. 1.

—————————, *Beachcombing*, p. 21. □

Silent guardians of the Oregon beaches use four-wheel-drive trucks, jeeps, pickups, in addition to standard patrol cars.

NOTES FOR CHAPTER 10:
WHO BUT THE JAPANESE ARE MAKING FLOATS ?

Webber, *Beachcombing*. p. 18

Wood (Binford), pp. 97-118

Information on the Oriental languages was obtained from Mrs. Hubert L. (Haruyo Kobayashi) Hatchell, Medford Oregon, then reinforced by *Britannica III,* Macropaedia Vol. 10. Chinese and Japanese: pp. 95-96; Korean: 529-530. □

NOTES FOR CHAPTER 11:
HOW MANY FLOATS STILL IN THE SEA ?

Webber, *Beachcombing,* p. 15.

Wood (Binford), p. 118 □

NOTES FOR CHAPTER 12:
EXPERIENCES WHILE BEACHCOMBING

Rasmussen, Margaret L. *Ocean Shores.* (Friends of the Library, Ocean Shores, Wash.) 1974.

Webber, *Bayocean   Salishan.*

_____, *RETALIATION:* Estevan incident, pp. 36, 38-40, 53; beach patrols, 79-91, 166; shell incident of 1973, 161.

Webber, [Eb]bert T. "Fishing Floats and Currents" in *Sea Frontiers* (International Oceanographic Foundation) Vol. 16, No.1 Jan.-Feb. 1970, pp. 26-31, 63.   □

NOTES FOR CHAPTER 13:
ヤシの実奇跡
Miracle of the Coconut

Webber, *Bayocean,* pp. 14-15.

The translation of the *Yomiuri Shimbun* article was done by Haruyo Hatchell of Medford, Oregon. The copy of that newspaper was supplied by Mr. Sadao Adachi, Tokyo, who also arranged for the use of the photographs. Mr. Adachi was a meteorologist during the Pacific War and did extensive upper air evaluations in preparation for the balloon bombing attacks on the mainland of North America, *which see* in Webber, *RETALIATION:* ... Chapters IX-XI. □

NOTES FOR CHAPTER 14:
DRIFTWOOD OF ALL KINDS AND SIZES

Holcomb, Jerry K. *Make it with Driftwood.* Driftwood House, Brookings, OR
   97415. Rev. Ed. 1975.

Schaffer, Florence M. *Driftwood Miniatures,* Hearthside, 1967.

Sommer, Elsye and Mike. *Creating with Driftwood and Weathered Wood.*
   Crown, 1974.

Wakeman, Harold. "Wakeman Art, Medium: Tumblewood," in
   Descriptive Comments (brochure). West Los Angeles, Calif. n.d.

Continued

There has been conjecture that the burning of salt impregnated ocean driftwood in home wood stoves may cause damage to the stove. Discussions between the authors and O.S.U. Extension Agents and with manufacturers of wood-burning stoves reveals there is the academic possibility that salt might damage some stoves under some conditions. Salt burns hotter than wood and salt is sometimes used in wood-burning stoves to blast out a clogged chimney. Damage to cast iron stoves is generally from burning too hot a fire too long (with any kind of wood) thus the iron might warp. Warping of iron fireplace grates due to oversize and too long burning a fire is common. Older iron stoves run risk of burning out because of deteriorated condition of the iron when compared with modern steel plate (Fisher) home wood stoves which are fire brick lined. To burn damp, salt impregnated driftwood or any green-cut wood over long periods of time may cause flu clogging. ☐

NOTES FOR CHAPTER 15: (None)

Examples (pages 183-185) of the countless numbers of ways to use driftwood as. art. "Tumblewood" art (p. 183). Flat driftwood (top, p. 184) became base for artist's brush. White glue used to attach bits of twigs. Carefully selected and polished driftwood (left) is made into design of potted plant then framed. Burlap is the background. (Right page) Selected woods have been cut then pieced together to form a picture. Technique is called "marquetry," defined as "thin pieces of wood cut to fit into other thin pieces so the color and grain forms a desired pattern or picture. Also, inlay of wood, ivory, etc."

Joe Harrod, Brookings, who created example shown, cuts wood 1/20th-inch thick. Back of picture (far right) labeled with name of each of ten woods used. Work is finished with Danish oil then occasionally wiped with furniture polish.

Woods used: avodire, curly maple, walnut, gum, holly, myrtle, purple heart, mahogany, plain maple, redwood burl.

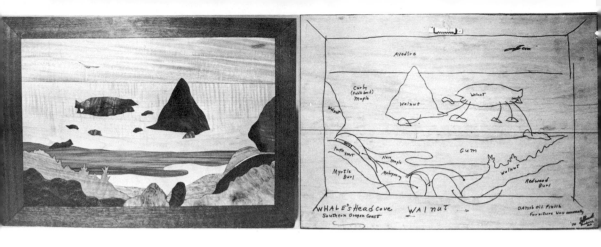

NOTES FOR CHAPTER 16:

KING NEPTUNE WANTS HIS SAND BACK

Byrne, John V. and William B. North. *Landslides of Oregon: North Coast.* Oregon State Univ. Dept. of Oceanography, 1971.

Schlicker, Herbert G. *et al.* "Environemtal Geology of the Coastal Region of Tillamook and Clatsop Counties, Oregon," in *Bulletin No. 74.* State of Oregon Dept. of Geology and Mineral Industries, July 1972.

Shepard, pp. 367-368.

Webber, *Bayocean—Salishan,* p. viii. □

NOTES FOR CHAPTER 17:
ROCKHOUNDING ALONG NORTHWEST BEACHES

Allen, John F.. *First Aid to Fossils; or What To Do Until The Paleontologist Comes.* [Bulletin No. 18] State of Oregon Dept. of Geology and Mineral Industries. 1939.

Browning, Clyde L. "Agate Varieties of the Pacific Northwest," and, "Oregon's Agate Beaches," in *The Agates of North America.* Lapidary Journal Pub. Co. 1966. pp. 15-19.

Moore, Ellen James. *Miocene Marine Mollusks from the Astoria Formation in Oregon.* [Geological Survey Professional Paper 149] U.S. Gov. Print Office. 1963.

——————————, *Fossil Mollusks of Coastal Oregon.* [Studies in Geology Number Ten] Oregon State Univ. Press. 1971.

Oregon Rocks, Fossils, Minerals; Where to Find Them. (pamphlet) Oregon Travel Information Div. Oregon State Highway Dept. n.d. □

NOTES FOR CHAPTER 18:
CLAM GUNNERS AND LOW TIDES

Oregon's Captivating Clams. Oregon State Univ. Extension Service, Sea Grant Marine Advisory Program, Oregon Dept. of Fish and Wildlife [pamphlet S.G. 28] June 1976.

Washington State Shellfish. Washington Dept. of Fisheries [pamphlet] June 1976.

Continued—

Wilkerson, Burford. *Let's Clam in Tillamook County.* Tillamook County [Oregon] Chamber of Commerce and Tillamook County Court. n.d.

Most cookbooks list various recipies for preparing clams. Some the authors are familiar with are in *The Joy of Cooking,* Rombauer or by Becker, depending on the edition. ☐

NOTES FOR CHAPTER 19:
FINDING AND PRESERVING SEASHELLS

Coale, R.D. *Preparing Sea Shells for Display* (Publisher unknown) n.d.

McKay, Frances Peabody *Brief Guide to Shell Collecting* Outdoor World-Preston, n.d.

White, James Seeley *Seashells of the Pacific Northwest* Binford & Mort, 1976.

NOTES FOR CHAPTER 20:
UNDERWATER BEACHCOMBING

James Seeley White provided the information and loaned the picture of the water-filled glass float. The infomation about his underwater experience in the "relic hole" is adapted from his article which appeared in *Oregon Journal,* August 13, 1976, p. 11, "Beneath the Surface: Relics Reveal Nahalem's Past." Mr. White also provided the photographs. For more information on old bottles and the patent medicines in them as used in Oregon, *see:* White, James Seeley, *The Hedden's Store Handbook of Proprietory Medicines* (privately published) 1974. ☐

NOTES FOR CHAPTER 21:
VICARIOUS BEACHCOMBING

Rammer, Alan D. "Beachcombing for Glass Floats" in *Pacific Search,* February 1977, pp. 36-37.

Webber, *Beachcombing,* pp. 16-17, 19-20.

Wood (Regnery), p. 176.

The breakfast announced as "8:00 a.m. to 11:30 a.m." that lasted most of the day (April 2, 1967) at Margaret Atherton's Tolovana Park House was hosted by Margaret Atherton, Marion Crowell and Billie Atherton Grant. The theme of the get together was, "Here shall he see No enemy But winter and rough weather"—Shakespeare, *As You Like It,* "Under the Greenwood Tree" Act 2, Scene 5. A pennant, with a drawing of King Neptune's trident, waved in the breeze from a flag pole in the yard. According to the memories of Margaret Atherton, Bert and Margie Webber and Sam and Betty Foster, confirmed by the diary of Amos Wood, there were twenty-six persons in and out during the day. Some of these have continued their interest in holding public displays of beachcombed materials and are active participants, either as committee members or as demonstrators/lecturers, each year at Seaside. Others, who became disenchanted with the magnitude of the Seaside event have withdrawn but are undoubtedly still beachcombing. ☐

★　　★　　★　　★

REFLECTIONS

Such beautiful therapy, the ocean.

I came here to reclaim something of myself for myself.

I've given away too much of myself far too long.

I came here to prove I can be on my own and feel comfortable with just me.

I've tramped and beachcombed many miles these past few days for the sheer joy of smelling fresh salt air, wading at the edge of the frothy tide, contemplating the curl of every wave, laughing at the antics of the playful sea otters bobbing and barking just beyond the edge of the surf.

I've felt my own mood and spirits lift and soar as I watched gull after gull ride the ever present wind. The flurry of the sandpipers at the water's edge caught my eye; let them be the busy ones I mused.

Today I need to watch it all and listen to my feelings.

God seems so close and prayer comes easily from heart to lips.

I rejoice in the glory and wonder of my reawakening.

The smell, the taste, the touch of the wind and the rain engulf me as the ocean engulfs the rocky outcropping below my feet.

There may be other days, other colors, other moods by the constantly moving, changing ocean. Today I feel a part of the soft shades of gray that surround me — the cloudy sky, the reflecting sea, the sandy shore.

The colors are soft and muted but alive. I feel an overwhelming sense of tranquility.

I feel clean and refreshed.

I've beachcombed without finding treasure; no agates or sand dollars, no shells or fishing floats, no driftwood I could carry. But I've found a new sense of peace I'm taking home to tide me over until I can return to the ocean.

Oh Lord, help me to hold on to what I have learned these past few days.

I'm ready to go home again.

M.W.

ILLUSTRATION CREDITS

Most of the photographs were taken by the authors and processed by them in their photolab. Extra assistance was provided by Dale B. Webber and Eugene B. Olson. Other photographs and illustrations are credited by page number.

INDEX

(Note: listings in *italic* are illustrations)